1987 Chair of Christian Thought
Lecture Series = U. of Calgary
= supported by Calgary churches

— p.78 the conviction w informs these
pages " good conclusion 92-3

CHRISTIAN FAITH
AND SOCIETY

— great R R strike of 1877? — S

— the Canadian scene = we have to guess at that. 27-8

— section on Evangelicalism quite
incompetent = no definition = obviously
borrows definitions + judgments from
surveys. = esp Marsden
esp 34-5: on inadequacy of
Evang'ism/fund'ism for social
action
= utterly at sea with evangelical
compounded contradictions, con...

— incompetent editing = innumerable
errors of punctuation esp'lly

CHRISTIAN FAITH AND SOCIETY

Gordon Harland

The University of Calgary Press

ISBN 0-919813-62-3

The University of Calgary Press
2500 University Drive N.W.
Calgary, Alberta, Canada T2N 1N4

Canadian Cataloguing in Publication Data

Main entry under title:

Christian faith and society

ISBN 0-919813-62-3
1. Church and the world.   2. Church and social
Problems.I. Harland, Gordon, 1920-
BR115.W6C57 1988   261.1   C88-091280-4

Printed in Canada

FOR RUTH

CONTENTS

Foreword

Preface

CHAPTER ONE Page

THE SOCIAL GOSPEL AND CHRISTIAN REALISM 3
The Social Gospel
Rauschenbusch's View of the Kingdom of God
Reinhold Niebuhr
Developing Concern
Niebuhr's Christian Realism
Examples of Niebuhr's Christian Realism

CHAPTER TWO

EVANGELICALISM AND FUNDAMENTALISM 27
Importance of the Movement
Understudied and Diverse
Fundamentalism
Historical Sketch
The Early Years
The Sixties
Conclusion

CHAPTER THREE

LIBERATION THEOLOGY 53
Historical Sketch
Themes and Characteristics
Ecclesial Character
The Preferential Option for the Poor
Liberation
Christology
Recurring Questions
Is Liberation Theology Marxist?
Violence
Critique
Conclusion

CHAPTER FOUR

CHRISTIAN FAITH AND THE SOCIAL TASK.......... 77
Pitfalls
Resources
Human Nature
The Distinctive Centre
Justification by Grace and a Political Ethic
Christian Conviction, Toleration and a Pluralistic Society
Realism and Hope
Conclusion

FOREWORD

The Chair of Christian Thought at The University of Calgary came into being as a result of the dedicated efforts of many laypeople who raised the funding required for the endowment of the Chair. Without the co-operation of the Calgary churches — Anglican, United, Presbyterian, Mennonite, Baptist and Roman Catholic — the Chair could not have come into being. The purpose of the Chair is to bring a leading thinker in the History of Christian Thought to The University of Calgary. While in residence at the University, the role of the occupant is to be a catalyst to both the University and the Church communities.

Gordon Harland, as the first occupant of the Chair, fulfilled the Chair's purpose in exemplary fashion. He gave graduate courses at the University and spoke in numerous Calgary churches. His most lasting contribution, however, was given in the form of the 1987 Chair of Christian Thought Lecture Series. This lecture series is offered annually and honours significant Calgary Church leaders: Louis Lebelle, Kaz Iwasa, Howard Bentall and Archdeacon Swanson. Dr. Harland's lectures evoked great response within both the University and Church communities. They are now made available for the wider scholarly and church community through their publication.

Harold Coward
Chair of Christian Thought Committee
University of Calgary

PREFACE

The chapters comprising this little book were given as public lectures at the University of Calgary in February, 1987, as part of the duties associated with the Chair of Christian Thought. The lively discussion these lectures provoked has led to the decision to make them available to a wider public. Except for minor editorial changes, the lectures appear as presented.

The current debate taking place in all Christian churches concerning the relationship between faith and society has determined the choice of topics. Since the questions being debated are deeply rooted in recent history, it seemed that a consideration of a few major movements directly concerned with the relation of faith and society might help to clarify the issues at stake. In the movements discussed — the American Protestant Social Gospel, Christian Realism, Evangelicalism and Fundamentalism, and Latin American Liberation Theology — particular attention is given to the ways in which the social message of these movements is correlated with the understanding of the work of Christ, human nature and history. The lectures make clear, I trust, the reasons for my conviction that the Christian faith possesses resources of insight into human nature and the dynamics of history which could make a significant contribution to the development of an adequate public philosophy in our time, as well as the view that these resources are frequently obscured in some current expressions of Christianity.

I wish to express my gratitude to the faculty of The University of Calgary, especially the Department of Religious Studies, as well as a large number of people in the churches of that city, for making my stay in Calgary so memorable. I also record my special thanks to Dr. Harold Coward, the Director of the Humanities Institute of the University, who so graciously chaired all the occasions at which these lectures were presented. I am grateful to Shelley Bozyk of the University of Manitoba and the secretaries of the Department of Religious Studies of The University of Calgary for their work in typing the manuscript and also to Linda Cameron and her assistants at The University of Calgary Press for their work in preparing it for publication.

Gordon Harland
Department of Religion
University of Manitoba
Winnipeg, Canada

CHAPTER 1

THE SOCIAL GOSPEL AND CHRISTIAN REALISM

A debate is raging in the churches. Sometimes it is fierce and frequently it is confused. This should occasion no surprise for it is a complex debate and it is concerned about issues of large importance. The centre of the controversy is the relationship between Christian faith and society. Something of the range and diversity may be quickly indicated by two or three specific references.

We mention first Liberation Theology in Latin America. This movement is regarded by many thoughtful people as one of the most heartening developments in Christian thought in our time; one of those creative movements in which Biblical understanding informs and sustains courageous witness and martyrdom in the name of the God who stands with, and for, the suffering and the oppressed. Other observers, equally thoughtful, sensitive and concerned, are persuaded that some expressions of Liberation Theology leave theology "without a substantive norm save the process of liberation itself."[1] Such critics are persuaded that this theology lacks a basis for making a clear distinction between the transcendent dimensions of faith and political enthusiasm or struggle. Two of the most distinguished and influential lay Catholic theologians on this continent — Gregory Baum in Canada and Michael Novak in the United States — have almost diametrically opposed judgments concerning Liberation Theology. At the other end of the theological and political spectrum is Moral Majority's combination of a fundamentalist, conservative religious perspective with a dedicated, skillfully organized political crusade which had some influence on the electoral success of Ronald Reagan in 1980 and 1984. Nor ought we to forget that in the Reith Lectures of 1978, Edward R. Norman charged that the most remarkable and distressing change to have taken place in Christianity over the past twenty years was the politicization of religion — "the internal transformation of the faith itself, so that it comes to be defined in terms of political values."[2] He issued a clear call to return to the recognition that Christianity is "by nature concerned primarily with the relationship of the soul to eternity...."[3]

As we contemplate this complex issue of the relation between Christian faith and society, we are faced by more than extreme movements of the right or the left. One thinks of the profoundly religious basis that moved a Dietrich Bonhoeffer to resist the tyranny of Hitler, and of Martin Luther King, Jr., who is best known as the greatest leader of the civil rights movement in America, but who perhaps should be viewed as the most charismatic religious leader in American history. Certainly King is not to be understood apart from the dynamics of the black evangelical religious heritage combined with his liberal theological education. Nor can one fail to mention the role currently being played by the American and Canadian Catholic bishops and their forthright engagement of economic and social issues.

The debate taking place is important for many reasons. The subject shapes the way in which the churches view their responsibilities, conceive their agenda, and to some extent how they allot their resources. It is important because it helps to give shape to their thought and feeling about what it means to be Christian and to participate in the Christian community. It is all this because the debate over the relationship between faith and society, between Christ and culture, is at bottom a debate concerning the nature of the Christian message itself. At the centre of this debate are those Biblical themes, images and doctrines which inform Christian views of human nature, the meaning of God's work in Jesus Christ, the social significance of this paradigmatic event, and the consequent interpretation of history.

Two movements which dominated the theological scene in America during the first part of this century — the Social Gospel and Christian Realism — are of considerable importance for this debate. They continue to inform Christian thought and action in the present scene and their respective views regarding human nature, history and the nature of the Christian message are central to the contemporary controversy. In our discussion, attention will be focused on the two greatest representatives of these movements - Walter Rauschenbusch and Reinhold Niebuhr.

The Social Gospel
The Social Gospel was one of the most creative movements in American religious history. Many factors conspired to bring the movement into being in the closing decades of the nineteenth century. It was a time of economic crises attended by intense and large-scale labor conflicts. The great railway strike of 1877, the labor disputes culminating in violent catastrophe in Chicago's Haymarket Square in 1886, the further strikes and industrial depression of the early 1890s were all vivid evidence that there were profound social dislocations in society clamoring to be engaged. It was a time of rapid urbanization, and succeeding waves of immigration. The "Perils of the City" were real and became a major item on the agenda of church conferences. The older evils of pauperism and crime, intemperance and vice were now joined by

industrial conflict, racial strife and the conflict of language blocs. It was also a time of railway scandals, government corruption and a general collapse of business ethics. It should not be thought, however, that the Social Gospel was merely the response to an external challenge. American Christianity had been dominated from the beginning by the passion to build a regenerated society so it was quite natural that its energies would be turned to confront the new situation. Moreover, these energies could now be guided by the new forward looking liberal theology with its emphasis upon the immanence of God working in and through nature and history to bring into being a transformed human community. All sorts of new forms were developed to give expression to the new concern: inner city missions, better training of the clergy in sociological matters, important conferences dealing with the issues, the establishing of chairs in colleges on "Applied Christianity," ecumenical cooperation in the developing of such organizations as the Federal Council of Churches, the publishing of papers, magazines and journals, and the popularizing of the movement through the Social Gospel novel, of which Sheldon's *In His Steps* was the most widely read. Before long there came another significant expression, the Social Gospel hymn which at its best gave poignant expression both to the range of human need and the depths of Christian compassion. A splendid example was Frank Mason North's hymn which came right out of his own experience:

> Where cross the crowded ways of life
> Where sound the cries of race and clan
> Above the noise of selfish strife
> We hear thy voice, O Son of Man.

The formative period also threw up a group of attractive leaders such as Washington Gladden, Richard Ely, and Josiah Strong. However, the most outstanding and influential exponent of the Social Gospel was Walter Rauschenbusch. This distinguished Baptist leader was born in 1861 in Rochester, New York. For six generations his forbears had been Lutheran clergymen in the pietist tradition until his father became a Baptist thoroughly committed to the evangelical heritage. Rauschenbusch himself experienced an adolescent conversion which affected him throughout his life. "It was," he said, "of everlasting value to me....It was a tender, mysterious experience. It influenced my soul down to its depths."[4] After study in Germany and at the Rochester Theological Seminary, he became a pastor in New York City on the edge of the area known as "Hell's Kitchen." Here this sensitive, intelligent young minister came face to face with the most pressing social problems of the age. Throughout his life Rauschenbusch was impelled by his evangelical passion but this confrontation with human misery meant that the individualism that marked his religious outlook was abandoned as he developed an inclusive social vision of a regenerated society which was centred in his understanding of the Kingdom of God. In 1897, Rauschenbusch accepted a teaching position at the Rochester Theological Seminary and ten years later he published a book titled *Christianity and the Social Crisis* which had a remarkable impact and was translated into several languages. The popularity which came overnight to Rauschenbusch was evidence that he had put his finger on a deeply felt need — the necessity to relate the Christian message to the full range of human experience, the social, collective life as well as personal morality and individual quests for salvation. Other important works followed, notably *The Social Principles of Jesus*, and of most importance to us, his final book, *A Theology for the Social Gospel*, published in 1917. He died in Rochester on July 25, 1918.

Rauschenbusch's thought was centred in a commanding vision of the Kingdom of God. In focusing his thought in this way he was not invoking a novel idea. On the contrary, this theme was deeply embedded in the American consciousness, and if we are to understand the peculiar power of this symbol of the Kingdom of God during the early part of our century, it is necessary to see the central role it had played in the American religious tradition.

In 1937, in his remarkably suggestive book, *The Kingdom of God in America*, H. Richard Niebuhr contended that the Kingdom of God had been "the dominant idea in American Christianity" from the earliest days to the time of his writing. It had, of course, meant different things at different times but it was, he said, "A New World Symphony in which each movement has its own specific theme, yet builds on all that has gone before and combines with what follows so that the meaning of the whole can be apprehended only as the whole is heard."[5] The theme had indeed been present from the beginning. For the essence of Puritanism was an intense experience of conversion that issued in an unrelenting zeal for the reformation of society empowered by the conviction that God was using them to revolutionize the course of human history. And a decade before this passion to build the holy community had broken out in revolution in England, it had gone on its errand into the wilderness of the New World, there to erect its "city upon a hill" that would be a model for all the world. This powerful heritage gained fresh impetus when it was fused with the revivalism of the Great Awakening with its vision of the new humanity, the new age and the new land. This contributed significantly to the ideology of the American Revolution and laid the basis for the developments of the nineteenth century in which America was viewed not only as a significant experiment in human rights — which of course it was — but above all as the Christian Republic which had been providentially raised up for the moral renovation of the world. The world of entrenched evil had been left behind in Europe with its kingcraft and priestcraft and America was embarked upon building the new humanity in the new Eden. Its hero became Adam before the Fall: "The world and history lay all before him."[6] However, this myth of the American Adam was, as R. W. B. Lewis remarked, "simply a formula for the way life felt to alert and sensitive Americans during the second and third quarters of the nineteenth centuries...."[7] The Puritan sense of divine calling and mission and the revivalists' version of the new humanity in the new age were now fused with a dynamic nationalism. With this development, that most powerful and persistent myth of the redemptive meaning of America was now fully adumbrated. It is that vision which reminds us of the truth of Richard Hofstadter's crisp remark that "It has been our fate as a nation, not to have ideologies, but to be one."[8] It is necessary to appreciate the depth of this theme in the heritage if we are to understand the power of the symbol of the Kingdom of God to gather up and focus the religious hopes and visions of Americans for the New Christianity and the new society in the early decades of this century.

Rauschenbusch's View of the Kingdom of God

For no one was the Kingdom of God more central than it was for Walter Rauschenbusch. Of particular importance was the way he connected this controlling concept with the prophets whom he described as "the beating heart of the Old Testament" and as indispensable "for any true comprehension of the mind of Christ."[9] It is interesting to note that Reinhold Niebuhr regarded this rediscovery of the prophets as teachers of social righteousness as one of the most significant achievements of the Social Gospel and of Rauschenbusch in particular. It was an achievement that Niebuhr thought deserved to be particularly valued and cultivated because of his own conviction that the Old Testament was an indispensable resource for the development of a viable Christian social ethic.[10]

Rauschenbusch was, however, particularly forceful in his articulation of the view that the Kingdom should be the ordering principle of all Christian theology. He was most explicit about this: "If theology is to offer an adequate doctrinal basis for the social gospel, it must not only make room for the doctrine of the Kingdom of God, but give it a central place and revise all other doctrines so that they will articulate organically with it."[11] The reason for such a demand is that it is "the marrow of the gospel," that which "occupied the chief place in the mind of Jesus." It is "the revolutionary force of Christianity" and, consequently, it is "absolutely necessary to establish that organic union between religion and morality, between theology and ethics, which is one of the characteristics of the Christian religion."[12] Therefore, to quote him again, "Any systematic conception of Christianity must be not only defective but incorrect if the idea of the Kingdom of God does not govern it."[13]

Rauschenbusch followed his own directive. In *A Theology for the Social Gospel*, he set forth his understanding of such major matters as sin, salvation, the church, the sacraments and eschatology in ways that are thoroughly governed by the controlling theme of the Kingdom of God. It is perhaps of some significance that the title of the concluding chapter of this work is "The Social Gospel and the Atonement." Sacrificial love was at the heart of his own view of the Christian life. The doctrine had frequently, particularly in the influential New England theology, been considered the chief Christian doctrine, and the American venture itself had been defined as Sacvan Bercovitch put it, "soteriologically."[14] Rauschenbusch thought, however, that "we are in a better situation to understand the atonement than any previous generation."[15] The reason for that was clear. While the individualism of previous ages had barred people from entering into the true meaning of the doctrine, our recognition of human solidarity puts us in the position of comprehending its true meaning. We can appreciate as never before that the sins which killed Jesus were public sins. Rauschenbusch discussed six of them — religious bigotry, the combination of graft and political power, the corruption of justice, the mob spirit and mob action, militarism, and class contempt — and stated that, therefore, the sins that killed Jesus were neither personal nor accidental, but "the reaction of the totality of racial sin against him" and also that "the guilt of those who did it spreads to all who re-affirm the acts which killed him." The key to the whole understanding "is contained in the realization of solidarity."[16] His discussion of the Atonement ends with the statement, "Thus the cross of Christ contributes to strengthen the power of prophetic religion and therewith the redemptive forces of the Kingdom of God."[17] The doctrine of the Atonement is important, but its significance lies in what it contributes to the task of prophetic faith. In Rauschenbusch, both its importance and its meaning were derived from the understanding of the Kingdom of God.

In Rauschenbusch, the Kingdom of God was a complex concept. On the one hand he urged that it "is divine in its origin, progress and consummation."[18] But this view was mingled with the immanentism and developmentalism of the progressive era. At times he talked so easily about the salvation of "super personal forces," and of organizations giving up monopoly power and coming under "the law of service." He even spoke of "saved" and "unsaved" institutions. But whatever his limitations, and the even greater shortcomings of his successors, the Social Gospel was a creative and humane movement that taught Americans in a fresh new way the social substance of all personal existence. There surely can be no doubt that the source of the achievement of the Social Gospel was the power of the symbol of the Kingdom of God to speak to a great range of needs. Through this understanding of the Kingdom the message of the prophets and the figure of Jesus received a new and attractive presentation; through the symbol of the Kingdom the divine activity and the mission of the church were tied to social history; through it personal piety and social passion were held together in a most dynamic way.

There were, however, serious weaknesses. The major flaw was that the Social Gospel was more a prisoner of the culture it sought to criticize than it ever knew. The reigning idea of progress, with its utopian view of history, meant that central matters such as the understanding of human nature, sin and grace, the person and work of Christ, had been emptied of much of their historic depth. And when this faith in progress to which the theme of the Kingdom of God was especially tied collapsed, then the movement's basis for creative social action was broken, and we have witnessed ever since the retreat into various forms of privatization and politicization.

Reinhold Niebuhr

Out of the Social Gospel and its collapse there emerged the towering figure of Reinhold Niebuhr who succeeded in a remarkable way in combining the religious depth of a theological tradition shaped by such figures as Augustine, Luther, Pascal and Kierkegaard with a tough minded, richly informed, social realism.

For four decades prior to his death in 1971, Niebuhr's influence had gone out in all directions. Rarely has a theologian achieved such respect from so many diverse groups. Writing in *The New Leader* a few months after Niebuhr's death, historian Arthur Schlesinger kept coming back to this question: "Why did this passionate, profound and humble believer have so penetrating an influence on so many non believers?"[19] Schlesinger found the key to Niebuhr's impact in the way in which he was deeply immersed in all the intellectual, moral and spiritual problems of the secular age while striving "for perspectives beyond them." It was not, Schlesinger added, "merely the extent to which the anguish of modernity informed his Christianity that accounted for his impact on the secular age. This impact derived no less from his powerful application of Augustinian analysis to secular questions."[20] Theologians, especially those who seek to contribute to the development of a public philosophy, owe more to him for thought and life than can readily be expressed. Political thinkers, particularly that school of political realists who possess a clear sense of the realities of power in collective life but who are also pulled by the claims of their religious and ethical commitments, found in him a particularly significant resource. Such people as Hans Morgenthau, Kenneth Thompson, Hubert Humphrey and Adlai Stevenson may be mentioned. Journalists, historians and literary critics all expressed their indebtedness to his thought and person. Among Jewish people he had a very special place, almost unique for a Christian theologian. One could mention the decisive influence he had upon Will Herberg's life and thought, the great friendship and twenty-five years correspondence with Supreme Court Justice Felix Frankfurter, and many other relationships. It is safe to say that no other Christian theologian was at that time held in such high esteem by the Jewish community. At Niebuhr's funeral, the distinguished Jewish theologian, Rabbi Joshua Heschel said of him, "He appeared among us like a sublime figure out of the Hebrew Bible....Revered, beloved Reinhold. In the words of the Psalmist:

> You are the fairest of the sons of men
> Grace is poured upon your lips
> Therefore God has blessed you forever.[21]

Richard Fox, in his biography of Niebuhr, summed up his far-ranging impact in these words: "the twentieth-century Christian church was shaken to its foundations by his piercing voice. So were the secular organizations of often agnostic liberals who flocked to him for inspiration. No one else could speak with such authority to Christian, Jew, and nonbeliever."[22]

Developing Concern
What then are we to say about the shape or thrust of Niebuhr's thought? We can get a feel for his concerns and the character of his thought by spending a moment observing his personal development.

It was as a young preacher in Detroit that Niebuhr rose to national prominence. He became in those years not only the beloved pastor of his congregation but also a virtual circuit-rider to the universities and colleges of America. It was here, in the pastorate, that he began to experience that crisis in his thought which was to have such consequence. He found that his theology lacked the depth to deal with the great mysteries and tragedies of life with which any minister worth his salt must somehow learn to deal. At the same time he was also finding that his liberal social gospel training was inadequate to deal with the economic and political conflicts of the community. He shared the concerns of the Social Gospel. Indeed in many respects he was more radical than the leaders of the Social Gospel. But although he shared its concerns and passion for social justice, it had three limitations which rendered it incapable of meeting the needs of the time. First, the Social Gospel's sentimental view of human nature meant that it could not properly attend to its own great concern - the problem of man in community. Secondly, it was politically defective in that it did not properly assess the reality of power and the power of self-interest. Thirdly, it did not sufficiently develop the theological foundations necessary to deal with the ultimate questions of life. These limitations of the prevailing liberal theology defined Neibuhr's task.   He would search, on the one hand, for an understanding of Christian faith that could speak with insight and hope to the ultimate questions of life, and provide resources for coping with the tragedies of our existence.   At the same time his task was to develop those resources of the Christian understanding of history that illuminate the dynamics of collective life.   His thought was rigorously whole.   He was ever the faithful pastor, dealing sensitively with the personal problems and deep hurts of human life.   The core of his theology was a powerful delineation of the Cross of Christ, as the suffering, sin-bearing love of God which is the sustaining ground of forgiveness and hope.   His thought remained always intensely personal, but he was never satisfied with a theology that could deal only with personal problems but which failed to come to grips with public issues.   His concern was to articulate an understanding of Christian faith that would simultaneously, and from the centre of the Gospel message, illuminate both the depths of personal life and the realities of our communal existence, including the conflicts of power in which we must be engaged if we are concerned to secure justice.

In 1928 Niebuhr accepted an invitation to join the faculty of Union Theological Seminary in New York.   For a man with his concerns, it was a propitious time to arrive there.   The central theme of his thought — the relationship between love and justice — would be vigorously engaged by the events of the next few years.   The harsh realities of the Great Depression were about to be experienced by everyone, and here Niebuhr developed, in an increasingly realistic way, the conviction that in the process of building communities every impulse of love must be transformed into an impulse of justice. These were also the years of the rise of totalitarianism in Europe. Most Americans were absorbed in domestic issues during those years, but developments in Germany received Niebuhr's close attention. They were years also of a widespread pacifism and of American isolationism. Niebuhr himself, like so many of his generation, had experienced a deep revulsion from the First World War and had become a pacifist. He broke with pacifism, however, because he thought it was blind to the demonic character of Nazism and also because in religious circles it was based upon what he considered to be a moralistic, reductionist understanding of the Gospel. It should be said that he always had a profound respect for the position of such people as the Mennonites, whose pacifism was part of their total spirituality, of setting down signs of the Kingdom of God in small communities. Such pacifism deserved support in a pluralist society. The kind of pacifism Niebuhr strongly criticized was that which presented itself as a political solution in the face of the Nazi horror. When some representatives of this position joined forces with isolationists and "America Firsters" who did not have an idealistic bone in their bodies, he snorted that this was not the foolishness of the cross, but just damned foolishness. In 1952, he suffered a series of strokes which resulted in partial paralysis. But still he learned. He had always been a gracious man and now that side of his nature deepened and mellowed. This is evident in an address to the graduating class of the Union Theological Seminary in 1957:

> If I have any regret about my early ministry it is that I was so busy being what I thought to be a prophet of righteousness, that I was not sufficiently aware of the pastoral ministry to the maimed, the halt and the blind, in short to all people who had to resign themselves to the infirmities of the flesh and who must finally face the threat of extinction.[23]

This serves to remind us of the wholeness and balance with which he approached the question of the nature of human nature and the range of human need.

Niebuhr's Christian Realism

Niebuhr's thought is best described by the label "Christian Realism." The term suggests an engagement between moral ideals and human recalcitrance, a profound understanding of both sin and grace, of the capacity of human beings for both good and evil. The Christian Realism of Niebuhr is not some hard, fixed position. Indeed, as Robert C. Good succinctly put it, Niebuhrianism, if there is such a thing, is

> Not so much a system of thought as a caste of mind. It is a complex of perspectives that, for Niebuhr, have been biblically derived and validated by experience - perspectives about human nobility and sin; human anxiety and the quest for security through power; the ambiguous role of reason, morality and religion, the nemesis of pride and power; and the persistent disturbing intervention of a Divine 'oughtness' in human undertakings.[24]

Niebuhr's Christian Realism likewise informed his critique of alternative positions. He agreed with the realists in their appreciation of the power of self interest in collective life, but he disagreed with cynics who not only take self interest into account but assume that that is the only thing operative. He agreed with idealists who understand that love is the law of our life and that in both personal and social life we need to be drawn out of ourselves and saved from the destructive consequences of self-centredness. However he found it difficult to abide the sentimentalist who not only takes love into account but thinks it can be readily realized in group life if only we have the will. A viable Christian social ethic, he constantly urged, was marked by a strong sense of responsibility to realize the greatest possible measure of justice in the concrete situation, and an understanding of human nature that freed us from both illusions and despair. Or as he said, toward the end of his life, that it had always been his "strong conviction that a realist conception of human nature should be made the servant of an ethic of progressive justice and should not be made into a bastion of conservatism, particularly a conservatism which defends unjust privileges."[25] Indeed, the central feature of his Christian Realism was its capacity to generate commitment to social justice while at the same time keeping us aware of the "taint of sin in the cause of our devotion."

Examples of Niebuhr's Christian Realism
The nature of Niebuhr's Christian Realism may be illustrated with reference to his views on democracy. He was firmly convinced that democracy had "a more compelling justification and requires a more realistic vindication than that given it by the bourgeois culture with which it has been associated in modern history." Certainly a free society "requires some confidence in the ability of men to reach tentative and tolerable adjustments between their competing interests and to arrive at some common notions of justice which transcend all partial interests."[26] But a too consistent optimism about human nature, a failure to understand the power and the persistence of sin and self-interest in life, and sentimental views about human perfectibility are perilous. Such an outlook had brought the great democracies to the brink of disaster as they faced the formidable tyrannies of Nazism and Fascism. He argued vigorously that a more realistic understanding of human nature, of our capacities for both good and evil, was required as a basis for democratic thought and life. He put his view in an oft-quoted epigram: "Man's capacity for justice makes democracy possible; but man's inclination to injustice makes democracy necessary."[27]
On the one hand it is the human capacity to reach out and affirm values of the common good, and to sacrifice for them, that makes democratic life possible. On the other hand the same Christian

understanding reminds us that no individual and no group can be good enough or wise enough to exercise absolute authority over their fellows.

In similar fashion, Niebuhr conducted an almost weekly analysis of the responsibilities that attended what he called "America's Precarious Eminence." The long heritage of conceiving herself as the innocent nation in a wicked world, together with the deep layer of messianic consciousness in the American mind, made it difficult for America to discharge the responsibilities of a hegemenous power. The heritage of the American myth of mission and destiny which prompts America to make a simple correlation between her power and her virtue, success and piety, affluence and wisdom, ill equipped her to deal with a world that has known so much suffering, poverty, frustration and defeat. It thus became a matter of passionate concern for Niebuhr to clarify those resources of Christian understanding and spirit most necessary for the task of enabling the United States to exercise responsible leadership on the international scene.

This took the form first of *unmasking* the deceptions and illusions to which America in her precarious eminence seemed peculiarly prone. The moral peril to which she was particularly prone was what Niebuhr called "the ironic tendency of virtues to turn into vices when too complacently relied upon; and of power to become vexatious if the wisdom which directs it is trusted too confidently."[28] A vertebrate Christian faith can *unmask* these ironic tendencies because of the way in which it believes "that the whole drama of human history is under the scrutiny of a divine judge who laughs at human pretensions without being hostile to human aspirations.[29]

Niebuhr was a realist but he was decidedly a Christian realist. His affirmations about God shape his understanding of the moral life and public philosophy. His social ethics and theological affirmations cohere together in a remarkably close and illuminating way. As we have seen his understanding of the transcendence of

God served as a vantage point of judgment in which human activities can be seen in both their value and their limitations. But God is not just a transcendent norm of judgment. For the Christian it is in Jesus Christ that we have the decisive disclosure of God. This means the disclosure of an inexhaustible divine love that takes our sin into itself and still loves, still accepts even our rejection of that love. The Christian affirmation is that here we have the revelation of the ultimate reality in all that is. It means further that when Christians think out from this centre of the suffering sin-bearing love of God revealed in the Cross, they will not be "beguiled by what is good in human existence into a false optimism and by what is tragic into despair. The message of the Son of God who dies upon the Cross, of a God who transcends history and is yet in history, who condemns and judges sin and yet suffers with and for the sinner, this message is the truth about life."[30]

It is from this centre of the Christian faith — in its basic evangelical doctrines of incarnation, atonement and justification — that Niebuhr developed his theology of history and it is this core which provided the basis of his political theology. He was most explicit about it: "This doctrine of Atonement and justification is the 'stone' which the builders rejected' and which must be made 'the head of the corner.' It is an absolutely essential presupposition for the understanding of human nature and human history."[31] This sweeping statement, so arresting in its boldness, is certainly not the sort that one is conditioned to expect from a thinker renowned for his political analysis. But this doctrine was so indispensable to Niebuhr because it affirmed so many important things for the life of Christians in the world. It presents humanity in all our complexity, our possibilities and our limitations, our grandeur and our misery. At the same time it discloses how the divine love takes our sin into itself and conquers it there, without abrogating the distinctions between good and evil upon which every healthy society depends. From this centre, too, Niebuhr developed the combination of realism and hope that marks the biblical understanding and which surely is a resource much needed by our frightened and frightening world.

We began our discussion of Niebuhr with Arthur Schlesinger's question: why did "this passionate, profound and humble believer" have "so penetrating an influence on so many non-believers?" Schlesinger concluded that it lay in Niebuhr's "capacity to restate historical Christianity in terms that corresponded to our most searching modern themes and anxieties."[32] That is correct. In Niebuhr's thought the passionate quest for meaning in life and for social justice was joined with a tragic sense of life. But the distinctive thing about his thought was the way in which these themes of our time were placed in the illuminating, healing and hopeful context of a Christocentric faith.

A debate is raging in the churches. It is over the relationship between faith and society, Christ and culture; at bottom it is a debate concerning the nature of the Christian message itself. The compassionate vision of Walter Rauschenbusch, the theology and social criticism of Reinhold Niebuhr, and the inspiration of both their lives, are a great resource for understanding the issues at stake.

Notes

1. See, for example, the discussion of Segundo's thought in Dennis P. McCann, *Christian Realism and Liberation Theology* (Maryknoll, N.Y.: Orbis Books, 1981), 222.

2. Edward Norman, *Christianity and the World Order* (New York: Oxford University Press, 1979), 2.

3. Ibid., 80.

4. W. Rauschenbusch, "The Kingdom of God," in Robert T. Handy, ed., *The Social Gospel in America 1870-1920* (New York: Oxford University Press, 1966), 265.

5. H. Richard Niebuhr, *The Kingdom of God in America* (New York: Harper, 1959), 164.

6. R.W.B. Lewis, *The American Adam: Innocence, Tragedy and Tradition in the Nineteenth Century* (Chicago: The University of Chicago Press, 1955), 5.

7. Ibid., 154.

8. Quoted in Hans Kohn, *American Nationalism* (New York: Collier Books, 1961), 25.

9. Walter Rauschenbusch, *Christianity and the Social Crisis* (New York: MacMillan, 1907), 3.

10. See Reinhold Niebuhr's article, "Walter Rauschenbusch in Historical Perspective," in Ronald H. Stone, ed., *Faith and Politics* (New York: George Braziller, 1968).

11. Walter Rauschenbusch, *A Theology for the Social Gospel* (New York: MacMillan, 1919), 131.

12. Ibid., 131, 133, 135, 140.

13. Ibid., 138.

14. Sacvan Bercovitch, *The Puritan Origins of the American Self* (New Haven: Yale University Press, 1975), 109.

15. Rauschenbusch, *A Theology for the Social Gospel*, 244.

16. Ibid., 259.

17. Ibid., 279.

18. Ibid., 139.

19. Arthur Schlesinger, Jr., "Prophet For A Secular Age," *The New Leader*, 24 January 1972, 11.

20. Ibid.

21. Quoted in Richard Fox, *Reinhold Niebuhr; A Biography* (New York: Pantheon Books, 1985), 293.

22. Ibid., 292.

23. Reinhold Niebuhr, "The Security and Hazard of the Christian Ministry," *Union Seminary Quarterly Review*, 13, no. 1 (November 1957), 21.

24. Robert C. Good, "Reinhold Niebuhr: The Political Philosopher of Christian Realism," *Cross Currents* (Summer, 1961): 265.

25. Reinhold Niebuhr, *Man's Nature and His Communities* (New York: Charles Scribner's Sons, 1965), 24ff.

26. Reinhold Niebuhr, *The Children of Light and the Children of Darkness* (New York: Charles Scribner's Sons, 1944), x.

27. Ibid., xi.

28. Reinhold Niebuhr, *The Irony of American History* (New York: Charles Scribner's Sons, 1954), 133.

29. Ibid., 155.

30. Reinhold Niebuhr, *Beyond Tragedy* (New York: Charles Scribner's Sons, 1937), 20ff.

31. Reinhold Niebuhr, *The Nature and Destiny of Man* (New York: Charles Scribner's Sons, 1941), v.1, 148.

32. Schlesinger, "Prophet for a Secular Age," 12.

CHAPTER TWO

EVANGELICALISM AND FUNDAMENTALISM

"There are three indisputable facts about the evangelical tradition in America. First, it is important. Second, it is understudied. Third, it is diverse."[1] So wrote Leonard I. Sweet in a brilliant article titled "The Evangelical Tradition in America" in which he detailed and assessed the historiography of the movement.

Importance of the Movement
The evangelical heritage is important; it is of particular significance for the relationship of Christian faith and society. It is important not only for Americans, where its impact is so visible, but also for Christians in many parts of the world. Although its influence on the Canadian scene cannot be precisely measured, everyone would agree that it has been substantial, pervasive and continuous. In this chapter discussion is confined to the American experience, in order to better manage a complex story but the relevance of the American

evangelical movement to the Canadian scene and elsewhere will, we trust, be evident.

Evangelicalism has been of great significance in American history. To think of the evangelical experience at the heart of the Puritan tradition, the influence of the Great Awakening of the eighteenth century with its emphasis on the new man in the new age, the dynamic heritage of the revivals of the nineteenth century in the cities as well as on the frontier or the role that evangelical experience has played and continues to play in the American South — just to mention these aspects of the American heritage is to realize the significant role played by Evangelicalism in the shaping of American. Richard Niebuhr saw this clearly fifty years ago:

> In other lands of Christendom, it may be possible
> to ignore the Christian revival of the eighteenth
> and nineteenth centuries....For America, however
> — the land of Edwards, Whitefield, the Tennents,
> Backus, Hopkins, Asbury, Alexander, Woolman,
> Finney and all their company — such an attempt
> is impossible. It cannot eradicate if it would the
> marks left upon its social memory, upon its
> institutions and habits, by an awakening to God
> that was simultaneous with its awakening to
> national self-consciousness.[2]

The people mentioned by Richard Niebuhr were all white. But the evangelical heritage has been even more central to the black experience in America. It should be stressed, however, that it was a distinctive form of Evangelicalism that was developed by the black people of America, one that stands as a strong reminder for the rest of the evangelical tradition of the resources for social change and criticism that inhere in the evangelical experience. Albert Raboteau has reminded us in his great work on *Slave Religion* that "In the midst of slavery, religion was for slaves a space of meaning, freedom and transcendence."[3] The story of the Exodus became the story with which slaves identified. They made it their own myth, and it in turn gave shape to their sense of identity as a people and provided them with an inexhaustible resource of dignity, purpose and hope. To the story of the Exodus they wedded the story of "Jesus Christ the Liberator" — the liberator from personal sin and social oppression. This personal appropriation of the drama of redemption — the heart of the evangelical experience — has remained the informing centre of black worship, which James Cone has described as "the actualization of the story of salvation as experienced in the lives of oppressed black people....Black people who have been humiliated and oppressed by the structures of white society six days of the week gather together each Sunday morning in order to experience another definition of their humanity."[4]

Black Evangelicalism is a distinctive and powerful articulation of the evangelical experience but it reminds us of how significant and pervasive the evangelical tradition has been in the whole American story. Such significance is not just a matter of past history; the current strength of Evangelicalism is everywhere acknowledged. R. Laurence Moore has reminded us that a Gallup survey in 1982 "reported that 35 percent of all adult Americans, not just church members or Protestants, claimed to have been born again in Christ; 45 percent had encouraged someone else to accept Jesus Christ; and 37 percent subscribed to the view that 'the Bible is the actual word of God and is to be taken literally, word for word.'"[5] Polls dealing with the nature of religious beliefs and experience must be approached with a healthy scepticism, but such matters as the statistics of church growth, the influence of the electronic church, the phenomenal success of evangelical publishing houses and the expansion of evangelical educational institutions, make it clear that Evangelicalism has long since left whatever cultural ghetto it was supposed to have been in and has become decidedly mainstream. Indeed the temptations and perils now facing Evangelicalism are those that have always confronted religious groups that are well established in a culture. In any event, the current religious situation in America forcefully reminds us of the importance of the evangelical tradition.

Understudied and Diverse

Leonard Sweet's statement emphasized not only that the evangelical tradition was important, but that it was also understudied and diverse. That it is understudied would seem to be true when one considers general histories and textbooks. But the situation in scholarly circles dealing with religious history is rapidly changing. This is demonstrated by the extensive literature which has recently emerged dealing with various aspects of American evangelical history. The increased work in the areas of black history and the role of women will also greatly enhance our understanding because of the intimate relationship both of these groups have had with the evangelical heritage. The most hopeful sign that the evangelical tradition will soon receive the kind of scholarly attention it deserves is the superior quality of the work of those now devoting their energies to it.[6]

The diversity of Evangelicalism is so great, and the history which has shaped its spirituality so complex that every historian dealing with it is faced with an enormous problem of definition. Who are we talking about? The problem may be indicated simply by reminding ourselves that most mainline liberal Protestant churches are rooted in, and still profoundly shaped by, the evangelical heritage. To turn in another direction, frequently Evangelicalism is viewed as embracing, as George Marsden, the distinguished historian of the movement, has noted, "black Pentecostals" and "strict separatist Fundamentalists" such as those at Bob Jones University, "who condemn Pentecostals and shun blacks."

The problem of diversity is such that one can readily raise the question whether we can properly think of Evangelicalism as a unified entity at all. George Marsden addressed this problem at length and made the helpful suggestion that several pitfalls can be avoided if we distinguish "three different, though overlapping senses in which Evangelicalism may be thought of as a unit." The first two ways of thinking of this unity are broad and inclusive.

First, Evangelicalism may be thought of as a term designating "a conceptual unity." In this sense evangelicals are those who are marked by certain doctrinal emphases and concerns such as the authority of scripture, salvation through personal trust in Christ, the centrality of a transformed life and an intense concern for Evangelism and missions. A second broad and inclusive sense is to view Evangelicalism "as a dynamic movement, with common heritages, common tendencies, an identity, and an organic character." The emphasis here is on the common roots, heritage and emphasis despite the fact of denominational diversity. The third way of thinking of Evangelicalism as a unified entity is much narrower. In this sense, Evangelicalism is not only a grouping possessing some common heritage and theological emphases but a real, self-conscious community. As Marsden put it, "It is a religious fellowship or coalition of which people feel a part." It is a quite self-conscious community which transcends denominational and even national boundaries, with people who have a true sense of belonging together and sharing a perspective and purpose. So both in the broader sense and in this more self-conscious way Evangelicalism may be regarded as a single movement, despite its diversities.[7]

Fundamentalism

Thus far we have spoken of Evangelicalism, without mentioning the familiar term Fundamentalism. There is a real relationship between them but it is historically a very complex one. Richard Quebedeaux rightly protested that "For too long it has been the fault of mainstream Ecumenical Liberalism to lump together with pejorative intent *all* theological conservatives into the worn Fundamentalist Category."[8] Such lumping together may sometimes be made with pejorative intent but it frequently is made out of ignorance or honest confusion. Whatever the reason, however, it is important to make the distinction because "in general, Evangelicals resent being called Fundamentalists, and

Fundamentalists likewise do not usually appreciate the Evangelical designation."[9]

The best definition of Fundamentalism is the one provided by George Marsden. He says that in order to understand Fundamentalism we should see it "as a distinct version of evangelical Christianity"[10] or more precisely as a "militantly anti-modernist Protestant evangelicalism."[11] He expanded this definition by saying that "fundamentalists were evangelical Christians, close to the traditions of the dominant American revivalist establishment of the nineteenth century, who in the twentieth century militantly opposed both modernism in theology and the cultural changes that modernism endorsed." He spelled this out by saying that "Militant opposition to modernism was what most clearly set off fundamentalism from a number of closely related traditions, such as evangelicalism, revivalism, pietism, the holiness movements, millenarianism, Reformed confessionalism, Baptist traditionalism, and other denominational orthodoxies."[12] It is a good definition because it locates both that cluster of movements with which it is related and its own distinctiveness. This definition also reminds us that some understanding of the historical development of Evangelicalism and Fundamentalism and particularly their changing relationship to American culture is necessary if we are to gain insight into the dynamics of the total movement.

Historical Sketch

The Early Years
Christianity confronted a series of traumatic challenges during the closing decades of the nineteenth century — Darwinism, a new understanding of history, Biblical criticism, urbanization and industrial dispute. The different responses of Christians to this new age represented a significant division with consequences that come down to the present day. On the one hand, Liberal theology and the closely allied Social Gospel represented a quite remarkable attempt to address the intellectual, social and religious issues of the new

era. They were impelled by the desire to claim this world for Christ and they were sustained in their labors by a commanding vision of a transformed world. Liberal theology was a creative movement and its many achievements deserve to be celebrated. The gravest weaknesses of this liberalism arose from the degree to which it was a religious version of the progressivist philosophy of the time. Because its view of human nature was often sentimental, and its confidence in the culture too uncritical, many of the grand themes of the Christian heritage receded into the background and the "Drama of Redemption" lost much of its meaning and immediacy. Many Christians thought that the liberal attempt to address the new age had been a virtual capitulation to the age, resulting in a profound erosion of the message of salvation. For such people liberal theology was thus a programme for the shipwreck of faith. To them, the so-called "higher criticism" bordered on the blasphemous, the progressive view of history meant a denial of Biblical eschatology, and the loss of traditional absolutes meant that the culture was awash in relativism. Drawing on such resources as the nineteenth century Princeton theology of Charles Hodge and Dispensationalism, which gained a wide readership through the *Scofield Reference Bible*), they launched a militant attack on the "Modernist Apostasy" through a strong emphasis on such doctrines as the inerrancy of scripture, the virgin birth, substitutionary atonement and the imminent return of Christ.

For our concern for the relation of faith and society, no development in the evangelical movement during this period is as significant as that which has come to be called "the Great Reversal" — a dramatic reversal in the social concern, commitment and strategy of evangelicals. The powerful evangelical stirring known as the Second Great Awakening in the early part of the nineteenth century, with such eminent revivalist leaders as Charles Grandison Finney, was quite distinguished for its progressive social concern. The revivalist tradition stemming from Dwight L. Moody in the period following the Civil War still had some strong social concerns but increasingly these impulses took the form of charity rather than political action. The "Great Reversal" took place in the period from 1900 to 1930 "when social concerns dramatically disappeared or were at least subordinated to others."[13] It is indeed striking that the period of the rise of the Social Gospel and the decline of revivalist social concerns seem to parallel each other so closely. "Social Christianity" was increasingly regarded as such a central part of liberalism that increasingly revivalistic evangelicalism regarded such social commitment as part of the "modernist apostasy."

The consequences of this division have been of immense significance and have come down to the present time. I will mention two. The first concerns the nature of the fundamentalist vision of the good society. Marsden put it this way:

> fundamentalists emerged from the experience not so much without social or political views as fixated on a set of views that had been characteristic of middle-class Americans in the last years before the crisis occurred. Their social views were frozen at a point that had been the prevailing American political opinion around 1890, save that the fundamentalists of the 1920s had forgotten the degree to which their predecessors — and even they themselves — had earlier espoused rather progressive social concerns.[14]

This development is crucial for our understanding of Fundamentalism and some of Evangelicalism of the Reagan era.

The second consequence of this division is of a theological nature and must be a major item on the contemporary theological agenda. Since social action was now identified with modernism, with apostasy, evangelicals concentrated their own message around the believers' trust in salvation through the atoning work of Christ. They did it however in such a way that the centre of the faith was effectively limited to the personal quest for personal salvation. This tradition has still not developed the resources for understanding human nature and history that inhere in such central evangelical doctrines as sin, incarnation, atonement, justification and eschatology. The evangelical tradition will not be able to make the contribution to public philosophy that it should make until this task is properly undertaken.

The 1920s represented a traumatic decade for the fundamentalist movement. It was probably at its peak about 1924 and it seemed quite possible that it might secure control of the Presbyterian Church and the Northern Baptists. Then came the famous Scopes Trial, widely known as "The Monkey Trial" in Dayton, Tennessee. Technically the fundamentalists won. The jury found Scopes guilty of violating the Tennessee statute forbidding the teaching of evolution in the public schools. Actually it was a humiliating defeat for the fundamentalists which had a profound impact on the movement itself and not least of all on the popular images regarding it. One consequence of the Scopes Trial was the widespread notion that Fundamentalism was synonymous with rural, and especially, Southern backwardness. Quite the reverse had actually been the case; the major centres of Fundamentalism had been urban and northern. Nevertheless "the conflict at Dayton," as Laurence Moore put it, "did enhance, both among Fundamentalists and their opponents, the impression of a vast cultural split between two sorts of Americans. But that split followed geographical lines or even urban-rural lines only in the imagination of H. L. Mencken."[15] A movement which heretofore had claimed significant intellectual leadership was now regarded as thoroughly obscurantist, the object of ridicule and disdain. This experience combined with the failure to entrench their position in such denominations as the Presbyterians, gave strong impetus to the separatist impulse in the movement. The withdrawal in 1929 of their prestigious theological spokesman, Gresham Machen, from the Princeton theological faculty, to form a new institution, Westminster Theological Seminary, and the formation a few years later of the Orthodox Presbyterian Church symbolized the new situation and the new separatist spirit. Thus by the end of the 1920s it looked to liberals and secularists at least, that Fundamentalism had retreated to the fringes of the religious and cultural life where it belonged. Doubtless it would shortly disappear.

However, that is not what happened. Although Fundamentalism had left the major centres of theological life, throughout the thirties it began developing a whole network of institutions and programmes that would lay the basis for a powerful witness at a later date. One significant form that this took was the Bible schools that were begun across the continent, among them such schools as the Moody Bible Institute, Wheaton College, and Dallas Theological Seminary. They quickly demonstrated a knack for reaching millions of people through radio, notably Charles E. Fuller's program the, "Old-Fashioned Revival Hour", which became the most popular religious program on the air, and was heard on the 456 stations by the year 1942.[16] Radio proved to be a powerful instrument, encouraging the faithful, helping to provide the sense of a meaningful community and at the same time reaching out to great numbers of new people.

Something else was going on during these years which is important for understanding the present scene. These were years when fundamentalists and evangelicals generally were licking their wounds and nursing their grudges. The mentality of the "Outsider" was deeply felt. But of equal importance is the fact that the vision of "Christian civilization" had not been abandoned. Evangelicals and Fundamentalists may have been outside the mainstream of American culture but they were equally certain that they embodied true American values which were being undermined by the liberal, secular establishment. This somewhat paradoxical combination of believing that one is simultaneously an "outsider" and also the "true representative" of the culture is one which produces tremendous energy and commitment. The dynamics of this combination have been a significant feature in the cultural and political life of the United States for the past decade.

The year 1942 marked another milestone in this history, with the formation of the National Association of Evangelicals (NAE), a fellowship designed to speak as one voice for conservative Protestants. The aim was to shake off the fundamentalist protest mentality and to shape a positive programme. The term "evangelical" was selected because it was a much richer and positive designation than the word "fundamentalist." As Quebedeaux put it, Evangelicalism distinguished the movement "from the extreme separatism, bad manners, obscurantism and anti-intellectualism so characteristic of Fundamentalism, but not from the Fundamentalist insistence on the authority and inspiration of Scripture, the necessity of conversion, and the mandate of evangelism."[17] From the outset Carl McIntire and other fundamentalist separatists denounced this development as a new capitulation to "ecumencial liberalism." The New Coalition represented by the NAE expanded, however, in a number of significant ways. The rise to prominence of Billy Graham as the leading American evangelist, in the tradition of Finney and Moody, the establishment of such schools as the Fuller Theological Seminary, and the launching of a new fortnightly journal, *Christianity Today,* were only a few high points in this period of renewal that marked the forties and fifties.

The Sixties

The events of the sixties and early seventies affected the entire culture in many profound ways. It was a period of great significance for all the churches. An important analysis of the religious situations of this period has been provided by Leonard I. Sweet in an article titled "The 1960s: The Crises of Liberal Christianity and the Public Emergence of Evangelicalism."[18] Sweet began his analysis by taking into account the fact that there were really two sixties. The first period, which ran roughly from 1960 to 1967, was marked by hope, optimism and buoyancy. The favorite adjective was "new." Sweet reminded us of how pervasive this mood was:

The phrase most characteristic of the spirit of this first sixties was the civil rights slogan 'We shall overcome' was a 'new optimism' (William Hamilton) expectantly labored for what some called a 'greening of America' (Charles Reich) and others a 'new Pentecost' (Harvey Cox), a 'new millenium' (Gibson Winter), a 'new world come of age', wherein could be found a 'new morality' (Joseph Fletcher), a 'new theology' (radical theology), a New Frontier (John F. Kennedy),...a 'new humanity' (Thomas Altizer)[19] and new cultures (youth, drug, and counter—). Even the "death-of-God" theology was announced in a mood of celebration.

The mood of the "second sixties" which ran from about 1967 to 1971 was almost completely the opposite. It was a time of broken dreams, increasing violence, wanton destruction and the expansion of the drug culture.

The period of the sixties and seventies was, however, also a period when Evangelicalism gained a whole new position in American culture. Its strength was so impressive that *Newsweek* and the Gallup Poll proclaimed 1976 as "the year of the evangelical." Sweet noted that by the mid 1970s evangelical Protestantism had "emerged with more vitality and resources than at any time since the Second Great Awakening 150 years before." This remarkable recovery in the "second sixties" must be seen, he argued,

against the backdrop of a dispirited and ailing conventional Protestantism that had little to declare theologically and was seldom able to answer even the simplest questions about the faith, to say nothing of answering them with a distinctive or strong voice. Into the vacuum created by this liberal 'mainline' Protestantism stepped a more conservative Protestantism that would become the 'mainline' religion of the 1970s. In short, evangelicalism came to function as a primary carrier of affirmations for an American culture otherwise in disarray.[20]

To many, this statement will seem rather harsh and perhaps somewhat unfair to mainline Protestant churches. However that may be, attention must be given to the reasons Sweet gave for such a judgment.

The two "sixties" were marked by crises of "authority" and "identity." It was Sweet's contention that "the umbilical connection between authority and identity has not been sufficiently elucidated," and that if the "religious developments in the 1960s are to be fully understood, an historical thematization that links issues of authority and identity must be forthcoming."[21] The "first sixties" was marked by a questioning of "old authorities and an embracing of new ones." The older liberalism may have uncritically accepted the authority of a scientific worldview but, "the liberalizing trend that characterized religion in the first sixties capitulated to the authority of a broader and more encompassing phenomenon of cultural secularization."[22] Partly out of apologetic concern and partly because of a loss of moorings, this "turn to the world" was distinguished by "an enthusiastic embrace of secularity." The nature of this trend seemed everywhere evident — in the "situation ethics" of Joseph Fletcher, in the widespread belief that the traditional framework of Christian thought had collapsed for good and that even thinking about "ultimate" or "religious questions" was a waste of time. Nevertheless it was buoyant in mood. This was the "Age of Aquarius." The church was generally regarded as irrelevant and the theology was divorced from the church and frequently set forth in abstruse language. Often it was absorbed in methodological concerns.

The new world looked forward to with such expectation in the early sixties did not arrive. What came for many people "was a vacant universe, a world where a living faith seemed remote and inaccessible and where people were left feeling abandoned and empty."[23] The new basis of authority in the culture had failed to fulfill its promise. The result was a new search for a satisfying basis in the self and in "human relationships." With the self as the authority, one's *feelings* became the ultimate criterion for everything: "Indeed, even the church became a place where people went to feel good about themselves."[24] With no large vision to command and no strong affirmations to be declared, it was a time when one's own ordinary experiences were "shared," and "listening" frequently became not a sensitive preparation for response "but the response itself."[25]

In this situation it was inevitable that issues of identity would come to the fore. Wherever one turned individuals, groups and institutions were suffering an "identity crisis." Sweet believed that:

> matters of identity became so important because the new basis for authority were destructive of identity... Lacking natural boundaries and a frame of reference within which individuals find their niche — a conception of self that corresponds roughly to the particular community's perception of self — a person becomes the victim of a diffused self image and suffers the sense of confusion that leads to personality dissolution and disintegration. In sum, problems of authority collided with problems of identity in the second sixties, and cult communes and psychiatrists' couches were strewn with the casualties of such collisions.[26]

The question of the relationship between identity and authority, or a framework of meaning and value, is important for our understanding of religious life at any time, and it is of special significance for this period. Several authors have discussed the significance of coherence, commitment and continuity in the establishment of identity. These three terms are crucial for the life of the Christian community, and the role they played, or failed to play, in the life of different religious groups is important for understanding the current religious scene.

The failure of American culture to provide the resources to establish identity had serious consequences for the religious scene. This failure was felt most acutely in liberal circles. Insofar as liberal Christianity had turned to the culture for its norms, it lacked the resources to meet the needs of the day. For one thing this "culturalist Christianity" was failed to provide the spiritual dimension needed to meet the yearning emptiness of a consumer society. The religious symbols had been so emptied of content that a meaningful religious interpretation of life and culture could no longer be provided. Liberal Christianity lacked, it seemed, the kind of theological framework to provide coherence for life. The absence of strong religious affirmations guided by a theology able to illuminate existence also meant that the power was lacking to energize the commitment and evangelical passion that had marked the liberal heritage. Indeed perhaps the gravest weakness of liberal Christianity was the loss of a sense of heritage, for nothing is more central to identity than the continuity provided by a vital tradition. Sweet did not exaggerate when he said "A tradition cannot long survive without a living memory. By failing to generate among church members a sense of living out of their past, much of Protestantism cut the cords of community in the present and endangered its survival."[27]

The relationship between the crisis of authority and identity in the culture and in the churches is necessary for understanding the present religious situation. It forms the context for the emergence of Evangelicalism to its position as a formidable force in American life since the 1970s.

This is, of course, not all that needs to be said. Liberals have stood firmly for many things that are absolutely essential to a faithful witness in our time. In the United States it was the leaders of the liberal churches who had the courage to stand firm and indeed be leaders in the civil rights crisis and in criticism of the Vietnam War. They have continued to exercise leadership in concerns for peace, human rights, the poor and ecological issues. They lost members through such stands but it is high time that they received acclaim for this witness. They contributed significantly to the Christian heritage by their action. In the process of dealing with large social issues, some painful and difficult matters that were hurting people in the pews may have received insufficient attention — and that is to be regretted — but nothing must allow the Christian significance of that social witness to be obscured.

By the mid 1970s the evangelicals and fundamentalists were deeply frustrated by the course of American culture. They were sure that something had gone terribly wrong. They were just as profoundly persuaded that they embodied the values for which America had historically stood, and for the first time in the century they sensed that they had the numbers and the momentum to do something significant about the situation. A whole series of events conspired to develop in them a sense of urgency: the Supreme Court decision in 1973 on abortion, the prohibition of religious exercises in public school, the demands and increased visibility of homosexuals, the availability of pornographic materials, and mixed in with this, the supposed decline of American military power and prestige in the world. The situation was one that called for concerted political action. Out of this situation were born the New Religious Right and Moral Majority. As Richard Neuhaus noted, for some time "the potent symbols and issues of patriotism, family stability and public decency had been permitted to gravitate to the Right."[28] The New Religious Right shrewdly exploited this situation and pro-life, pro-family, pro-morality and pro-America became the four planks in Moral Majority's platform.

We need note Moral Majority only in passing. It was born of a marriage of the electronic church and the direct mailers, those experts who specialized in securing money and political support for specific candidates and causes. The political campaign of this New

Christian Right became most visible during the election campaign of 1980 with its notorious "moral report cards" and "target lists." When even respected senators like Mark Hatfield, an evangelical and a Republican, scored low on the report card, many suspected that the operative criteria had been drawn not from the Bible or Christian thought, but from the agenda of the political Right. The cultural captivity of religous liberals was surely never as complete as this.

This cultural captivity of the new Religious Right demands theological assessment because it is here that one encounters some surprises. There can be no doubt that the strength of the whole conservative religious movement lies in the fact that it understands itself as centred in the Bible and concerned first and foremost with the message of the saving work of God in Jesus Christ. Surely its great appeal is a result of the way in which it has proclaimed the great affirmations of the Biblical message. Yet, paradoxically, it is also here where the movement is most disappointing.

This deficiency is to be noted in the presentation of several doctrines of the faith but we can deal here only with one. Perhaps nowhere is this inadequacy more visible than in the understanding of human nature, and quite specifically in the doctrine of sin. To be shaped by a Biblical understanding is to know that sin arises from a level that is deeper than conscious choices and actions. It is rooted in the centre of our beings, in the basic orientation of the self, in what it is that we really love, in what St. Augustine called "the gravity of the soul." The springs of sin are in a falsely centred self, a self inordinately attached to itself, and estranged from itself because it has thus disrupted the relationship with God in which it finds fullness of being. Moreover it is precisely the evangelical experience of conversion and repentance that illumines both the depth and pervasiveness of sin. No one should know more profoundly than the evangelical that this sinful condition marks all people and not just some people, and that saved sinners live by grace; that no matter what heights of virtue may be attained, there is no point where one is beyond the need for forgiveness. Indeed one of the marks of the redeemed is not that they are conscious of their virtue but that they have been freshly sensitized to their need for forgiveness for the degree to which they are involved in the pain and hurt of the world.

This understanding of the depth and pervasiveness of sin has made Christians realistic about personal and corporate life. It is a condition that affects all people. One social consequence has been a firm belief in the necessity of restraints upon every concentration of power. It is a basic conviction of Christianity and democracy that no person and no group can be good enough or wise enough to exercise absolute power over their fellows. One expects Biblically-oriented Christians to have a lively sense of this. But the New Religious Right, for all its Biblical language, has a most unbiblical view of human nature. For one thing, they put incredible confidence in the "righteous" man, the "strong" leader. They seem to have little sense of the dangers of concentrated power, either political power if it is centred in "approved" leaders, or the sort of power vested in their own charismatic religious leaders. The absence of adequate structures and processes of accountability in the case of television evangelists is a vivid example of this deficiency. The tragic realities of human nature so richly articulated in the Bible and the Christian heritage have been obscured. Instead we have here a Manichean view of human nature in which people are divided into the good guys and the bad guys, the white hats and the black hats, a view which owes much more to the legend of the American "Western" than it does to the Bible.

It is a small step from this perspective to what Gabriel Fackre has called "the greatest departure from Christian doctrine by the Religious right" namely its "functional elevation of America to the place of a chosen nation."[29] It is the role of Biblical religion to provide a framework of understanding and value that will prompt a nation to seek to realize the greatest possible social and cultural values and at the same time make the nation keenly aware of the "taint of sin in the cause of our devotion." It was this that Reinhold Niebuhr urged upon his fellow Americans over forty years ago: "Thus a contrite recognition of our own sins destroys the illusion of eminence through virtue and lays the foundation for the apprehension of 'grace' in our national life."[30] It is this sort of Biblical understanding that is lacking in the New Religious Right where an alien, "secular" approach has taken over.

Conclusion

What then is one to say about the present scene? Clearly it is so complex and fluid that to venture any predictions is a hazardous undertaking. Although the picture is far from clear it seems to me that two significant developments are taking place. First, it appears that the highwater mark of Fundamentalism has passed. Naturally, leading fundamentalists do not agree. Ed Dobson and Ed Hindson, associates of Jerry Falwell, opened their Preface to the second edition of *The Fundamentalist Phenomenon* with the bold assertion that, "As we predicted in 1980, Fundamentalism has become *the* religious force of the 1980s."[31] Certainly its strength is real, it has roots in the culture, and has always been able to generate strong commitment. It will survive. But there are several reasons for thinking its social and political influence has passed its peak. Fundamentalism can be strong only as it maintains a coalition with the broader evangelical movement, and only as long as it is widely perceived that the enemy, "secular humanism," controls the seats of power. There is no longer a fundamentalist-evangelical consensus. Even a conservative evangelical like Carl F. H. Henry, obviously with Falwell in mind, spoke dismayingly of those leaders who "with prophetic self-assurance will counsel evangelicals publicly to invest in South African Krugerands." Henry then followed his remark with the following observation and question: "Constituency confidence in mainline denominations waned notably as a consequence of ecumenical politicization. Are evangelical churches less vulnerable to such disaffection simply because their politicization would be on the right rather than on the left?"[32] Not only has the coalition upon which political success depends appear to have collapsed, but the experience of the heady days of success would seem to shake confidence. After all, remarkably little of the "social agenda" of the New Religious Right has been enacted by the Reagan administration in what Falwell called "this decade of destiny." Moreover the fear that the New Religious Right threatens the pluralism of America has deepened. There probably will always be tension between the vision of a "Christian civilization", which is deeply rooted in the American heritage, and the equally valued American tradition of religious pluralism. But because the particular vision of the New Religious Right has been so riveted on the late nineteenth century, it has become increasingly clear to the general public that implementation of its vision would result in an intolerable constriction of the reality of pluralism.

The second development taking place is a growing convergence of evangelical concerns with those of mainline churches and with the world of "liberal" theological scholarship. This is evident in several areas. Biblical criticism has taken strong root in evangelical circles and exceptionally able scholars are engaged in the effort to hold together the claims of faith and scholarly criticism. The experiential shape of evangelical piety has meant a convergence of many concerns with fellow liberals in the area of pastoral care. Evangelicals did not produce any successors to the theological giants of former years and there are many indications that they are ready now to make a fresh appropriation of such theologians as Barth, Brunner, Tillich, Nygren, Reinhold and Richard Niehubr who represented the greatness of what is sometimes called "neo-orthodoxy" but which would be better understood as "creative liberalism." Increasingly, evangelicals have also developed a social concern which has led some of them to a fresh appreciation of both "Christian realism" and contemporary Catholic thought.

Such a convergence deserves to be nurtured. If it took place Evangelicalism and the mainline Protestant churches would make the discovery that they have a heritage in common and that it is wonderfully rich. Evangelical experience and social passion, which should never have been separated, could again be united. And not least of all, these two strands might together do something which neither has been able to do alone — make a contribution to a much needed public philosophy which will protect and enhance human life in a perilous world.

Notes

1. Leonard I. Sweet, ed., *The Evangelical Tradition in America* (Macon, Georgia: Mercer University Press, 1984), 1.

2. H. Richard Niebuhr, *The Kingdom of God in America* (New York: Harper, 1959), 125ff.

3. Albert J. Raboteau, *Slave Religion: The "Invisible Institution" in the Antebellum South* (New York: Oxford University Press, 1978), 318. See also his chapter "The Black Experience in American Evangelicalism: The Meaning of Slavery," in Leonard I. Sweet, ed., *The Evangelical Tradition in America*.

4. James H. Cone, "Sanctification, Liberation and Black Worship," in *Theology Today*, 25, (July 1978): 148, 140.

5. R. Laurence Moore, *Religious Outsiders and the making of Americans*, (New York: Oxford University Press, 1986), 167.

6. Robert Moats Miller has remarked that "Today scholarly writing on Protestant fundamentalism in modern America is far more abundant in quantity and superior in quality to that on Protestant liberalism." Quoted in Sweet, *The Evangelical Tradition in America*, 75. The work of such authors as Marsden, Noll, Wacker, Hatch, Carpenter, Sweet (to name only a few) would support this judgment.

7. George Marsden, "Introduction: The Evangelical Denomination," in George Marsden, ed., *Evangelicalism And Modern America* (Grand Rapids: William B. Eerdmans, 1984).

8. Richard Quebedeaux, *The Young Evangelicals* (New York: Harper and Row, 1974), 19.

9. Ibid.

10. George M. Marsden, *Fundamentalism And American Culture The Shaping of Twentieth Century Evangelicalism 1870-1925* (New York: Oxford University Press, 1980), 3.

11. Ibid., 4.

12. Ibid.

13. Ibid., 90.

14. Ibid., 93.

15. Moore, *Religious Outsiders and the Making of Americans*, 160.

16. E. Dobson, E. Hindson, G. Falwell, *The Fundamentalist Phenomenon*, 2nd ed. (Grand Rapids: Baker Book House, 1986), 88. For the significance of the Bible Schools of the American scene see Joel E. Carpenter, "Fundamentalist Institutions and the Rise of Evangelical Protestantism," *Church History* 49 (March 1980) where he described how the Bible Schools "became the regional and national coordinating centers of the movement." (p.67) For the Canadian scene see Ben Harder's article, "The Bible Institute-College Movement in Canada," *Journal of the Canadian Church Historial Society* 22 (April 1980) and Ronald G. Sawatsky, "The Bible School/College Movement in Canada: Fundamental Christian Training," *Canadian Society of Church History Papers*, 1986.

17. Quebedeaux, *The Young Evangelicals*, 12.

18. This is Chapter 3 of George Marsden, ed., *Evangelicalism in America.*

19. Ibid, 30.

20. Ibid., 32.

21. Ibid., 31.

22. Ibid., 34.

23. Ibid., 37.

24. Ibid., 38.

25. Ibid., 42.

26. Ibid., 40.

27. Ibid., 43.

28. Richard John Neuhaus, "Who, Now, Will Shape the Meaning of America?" *Christianity Today* 19 March 1982, 20.

29. Gabriel Fackre, *The Religious Right and Christian Faith,* (Grand Rapids: William B. Eerdmans, 1982), 62. This little book is one of the best theological critiques of the "New Right" available.

30. Reinhold Niebuhr, "Anglo-Saxon Destiny and Responsibility," *Christianity and Crisis* 4 October 1943. This article is reprinted in Conrad Cherry's splendid work, *God's New Israel: Religious Interpretations of American Destiny* (Englewood Cliffs: Prentice-Hall, 1971).

31. Dobson, Hindson, Falwell, *The Fundamentalist Phenomenon,* xiii.

32. Carl F. H. Henry, *Confessions of a Theologian: An Autobiography* (Waco, Texas: Word Books, 1986), 397-398.

CHAPTER THREE

LIBERATION THEOLOGY

We live in a time of great religious ferment. In theological terms, the most momentous development of the past two decades has been the appearance of a great variety of liberation theologies. The attention they have received, the changes they have already effected and the controversy they have engendered attest to their energy and vitality.

They are challenging movements. One reason that makes these movements so challenging is geographical. Liberation Theology is a truly global development, focused in the Third World. This fact possesses an importance that has not yet generally penetrated our consciousness. In 1984, something happened of immense significance in the history of Christianity. For the first time since the second century, the majority of Christians were now living not in European-North American culture, but in what we call the Third World. Just to think of the liberation theologies coming from Latin America, Africa, Asia and the Caribbean as well as the black theologies of the United States and the worldwide feminist theologies, is to realize that the theological scene has been dramatically and permanently altered, regardless of the judgments that may have of their value.

The diversity of liberation theologies should not be overlooked. The term "Liberation Theology" has, however, been particularly associated with Latin America. There it has been given distinctive expression by a number of gifted and dedicated theologians. There, too, it has developed significant ecclesial roots, in what is called the "basic" or "grassroots" communities, the *communidades de base*. It is a very important movement for South America, for the Roman Catholic Church, and for all of us.

We may get some feeling for this massive movement by attempting three things:

1) a brief historical sketch of the development of the movement;

2) a discussion of some of the major themes and characteristics of this theology;

3) a consideration of some of the recurring questions and criticism of liberation theology.

Historical Sketch
In many ways it is a surprising thing that Latin America should be the source of one of the most socially progressive Christian movements in our time. The history of Catholicism on that continent has scarcely been such as to lead us to anticipate such a development. Throughout history, until very recent years, the Church has been a willing, dependent partner of the state. Penny Lernoux described the relationship this way: "In return for political servitude, the Church was given the right to arbitrate the social mores of colonial society and to inculcate the 'heathen' with a Spanish Catholicism still rigidly bound to the Middle Ages."[1] The men who transplanted Spanish Catholicism were, with a few notable exceptions, of rather low calibre but assured of their European superiority. As Lernoux put it: "Handicapped by a superiority complex, by laws and customs fashioned for European

Catholicism, and ignorant of the cultural heritage and values of the New World's indigenous peoples, most missionaries became 'vending machines of the sacraments.'"[2] The early invaders treated the Indians ruthlessly, although one bishop of the sixteenth century, Bartolomé de Las Casas, took the side of the Indians and has become a special hero in our time for Gustavo Gutierrez.

It is a harsh story. Despite the fact that 90 percent of the region's 320 million people are baptized Catholics, the real religion is "a syncretic religion, with a message of fatalism. Thus children do not die of malnutrition; it is God's will that they should die. Similarly, poverty is a condition of birth, not something that can be changed by individual or collective endeavor." Moreover, the Church which was used in the beginning as a "tool of conquest" has continued to play its role in founding and sustaining the social pyramid in Latin America which Lernoux describes as "a few white Europeans living in outrageous luxury while the mass of the people subsisted in misery."[3] With this came also a heritage of violence and disregard for human rights which forms the deeply rooted context of the situation today.

The situation as regards the Church began to change in the 1960s. The social teachings of the Catholic Church and some progressive currents set loose by Vatican II conspired with the frustrations and blighted hopes attending the "development programs" of the day, to set the stage for what Lernoux has called a "spring cleaning" in "the Latin American Church, the first such cleaning in history."[4]

The event which brought this "spring cleaning" to public expression was an important conference of the Latin American bishops held at Medellin, Columbia, in 1968. The topic of the conference was "The Church in the Present Day Transformation of Latin America in the Light of the Council." The importance of this conference is difficult to overestimate. Indeed it is not inappropriately referred to as the "Vatican II of Latin America," the most outstanding event in the life of the Latin American Church in this century. A commitment to the poor was made in that conference that was to be of the utmost significance. To be sure, most of the Medellin documents were the usual bland stuff. But those sections which attacked the prevailing social and political system and made a clear commitment to the poor and downtrodden took on a life of their own. Some of these sections, such as the following "pastoral points" were unambiguous: Point number 21 reads, "To awaken in individuals and communities...a living awareness of injustice, infusing in them a dynamic sense of responsibility and solidarity." Point number 22 continues, "To defend the rights of the poor and oppressed according to the Gospel commandment, urging our governments and upper classes to eliminate anything which might destroy social peace: injustice, inertia, venality, insensibility." And in Point number 27 we read, "To encourage and favor the efforts of the people to create and develop their own grass-roots organizations for the redress and consolidation of their rights and the search for true justice."[5] Everywhere people were astounded that so many conservative bishops could take the position they had, and indeed many bishops indicated that they had not realized what they had signed. But a distinguished group of prelates — such as Helder Camara, Aloisi Lorscheider and Paulo Arns — stood firm. Taking a strong position was a matter of great significance because:

> For all its defects and desertions, the Catholic
> Church is still a power to be reckoned with in Latin
> America, as much a part of society's fabric as
> Islam in the Middle East. As the only institution
> capable of withstanding the military, the Church
> has become a surrogate for democracy, providing
> a protective umbrella for popular organizations,
> such as labor unions and peasant federations,
> which otherwise would succumb to repression.[6]

The decade following Medellin saw the establishment of new strategies and structures to give expression to the new vision. Of prime importance was the widespread development of "grassroots" or "basic" communities. By the year 1979 there were 80,000 of these communities in Brazil alone. These small groups — of about fifteen to twenty people — engage in Bible study, discuss practical problems and plan strategies to face neighborhood needs. In this way religious understanding is integrated with daily life and the struggle for a better society. The Bible is viewed as a story of liberation and this understanding impels the participants to a transformation of those conditions which previously had been accepted in a fatalistic spirit. Children do not die because it is God's will but because of lack of food, medicine, and because of unsanitary conditions, all of which can be changed. The religious focus of popular piety undergoes a consequent redirection. The Cross is changed from a symbol of death and defeat into a symbol of redemption and victory. The prophetic spirit of Biblical witness is joined with a concrete participation in community action.[7] When these concerns are combined, we obtain some insight into the context, the sustaining communities and the practical, passionate concerns of Liberation Theology. Indeed, a definition of Latin American Liberation Theology may now be ventured. The Canadian Catholic theologian, Gregory Baum, who is also an articulate and ardent supporter of the movement, has provided us with a succinct definition: "it is an interpretation of the Christian message, generated by popular groups and articulated in systematic form by theologians, that brings out, in the Latin American context, the this — worldly, critical, transformist or revolutionary meaning of the divine promises revealed in Scripture."[8]

The decade following Medellin was, however, very complex. It was not at all easy going for the proponents of change. While the ideas of Liberation Theology was trying to set down roots, the movement faced a formidable campaign of opposition both from abroad and from within. The campaign involved German bishops, the De Rance Foundation in Milwaukee, a Belgian Jesuit, Cardinal Baggio in Rome, and was directed by the Latin American bishop Lopez Trujillo who had become the Secretary General of CELAM

(The Latin American Episcopal Conference). Since some German bishops were involved in the attack, it should be noted that their activities were strongly criticized by such eminent German theologians as Catholics Karl Rahner, Johannes Metz, Herbert Vorgrimler and Protestants such as Martin Niemoeller, Helmut Gollwitzer and Ernst Kasemann.

The Latin American Episcopal Conference, designed to be the follow-up to Medellin, was scheduled to take place in Puebla, Mexico, in 1979. The preparations for this conference became the focus of the struggle. A preliminary consultative document was prepared for the conference which made clear that the commitments made at Medellin were to be renounced. This preliminary document set off a grand international debate, in Europe and in North America as well as in South America. Moderate bishops met to recast the document. There were serious attempts to set the clock back to where it was before Medellin. The delegates appointed to the conference were heavily conservative: "Missing among the experts were all of Latin America's best known theologians: Gustavo Gutierrez, Juan Louis Segundo, Leonardo Boff, Hugo Assmann, Jon Sobrino, Ignacio Ellacuria, Raul Vidales, Enrique Dussel, Segundo Galilea, Pablo Richard, and José Comblin."[9]

Experienced bishops know, however, that there are many ways to manage a conference. Although they had been denied the opportunity to bring their own theologians and social scientists as advisors to the conference, the progressive bishops invited them to come along anyway. Although these experts could not enter the compound where the conference was held, they were put up in a convent three blocks away, and the bishops could not be prevented from going out to them. By working day and night these "outside theologians and social scientists were able to prepare eighty-four position papers for the twenty-one commissions as the document went through four drafts"[10] with the result that what began as a disastrous report turned into a minor victory. At least the worst prospects were averted. There is no condemnation of Liberation

Theology nor outlawing of what had been called "a parallel magisterium." Moreover the document repeatedly speaks of "the preferential option for the poor" which became a much publicized slogan and thus a retention of the commitment of Medellin. What was clearly visible at Puebla, however, and what has remained visible since is that the Church in Latin America has two faces — the popular Church, which in Brazil, has powerful episcopal support, and the traditional "strictly hierarchical" church.

Themes and Characteristics

Ecclesial Character

We have referred to the grassroots or basic communities, which meet, sometimes with a priest, frequently without, to share a liturgical life, engage in Bible study and tackle all sorts of local problems. Perhaps there is no more distinguishing characteristic of Liberation Theology than the relationship it bears to these communities. The relationship is close, intimate, one might almost say organic. The theologians have been well trained, mostly in European schools, but the basic communities provided the context for the movement. The American Protestant theologian Robert McAfee Brown puts it this way:

> Theologians like Gustavo did not muse, 'Here are all these new centers of church life, let us provide them with a theology.' The reverse was true: as people wrestled with their own problems in the light of their faith, a new way of *doing* theology emerged — not theology from the top down, but from the bottom up, from particular groups of people to all the rest of the people, with Gustavo and others helping to pull it all together so that it could be shared more widely.[11]

Liberation Theology has thus an ecclesial character because of its close relationship with these communities. This raises a very important question. These "basic communities" are discovering a new way of being church and they thus reopen the whole question of ecclesiology, that is, the nature of the church, in a dramatic new way. The core question has been recently asked by Leonardo Boff, "Are these communities themselves actually church, or do they merely contain elements of church?"[12] The answer given will surely depend on where one is coming from. Boff is emphatic, however, that the people involved in the communities "feel that they are in contact with actual, genuine church, and not just with ecclesial elements or parachurch communities."[13] He continues, "The Church abides in the people of God as they continue to come together, convoked by the word and discipleship of Jesus Christ. Something *is* new under the sun: a new Church of Christ."[14] Many important issues, of far reaching significance for the Church, are posed by the existence of these communities and they are addressed by Leonardo Boff in his recent work, *Ecclesiogenesis*. The immediate question is: What is the relationship of these communities to the grand institution of the Roman Catholic Church? It would surely seem that both need each other. On the one hand the "communities" cannot replace the parish, on the other hand, the "global" church faces the question of whether it will respond to this network of basic communities with its call for social transformation or whether it will keep, unmodified, its relationship with the existing social structure.

English religious history provides us with a remarkably close parallel: the Methodist revival of the eighteenth century with its vast network of societies serving the needs of so many victims of the Industrial Revolution. Marginalised people experienced a new and liberating understanding of the meaning of the church in the Methodist societies as they have done in the "basic communities." A lively study of the Bible and a fresh appreciation of its relevance to their condition has marked both movements. Likewise both groups have had a profound desire for the nurture given in the Eucharist and for both groups this yearning coincided with a dearth of duly ordained and willing clergy. For both groups this situation served to bring the question of the meaning of ordination and the relationship of the priesthood to the community of believers, sharply into focus. The question that Boff engages, whether the "basic communities" represent a real church or are merely groups possessing some ecclesial elements was the same question which faced the Anglican Church and the Wesleyan movement from the beginning of the Methodist revival. The issue whether the Methodist movement represented a real church or merely ecclesial elements came to a head in the American colonies where people were converted, gathered into societies where they were taught and nurtured, but who went for years without the sacraments. This situation provided the context for the separation of the Methodists from the Church of England. There is, of course, a vast difference in the historical analogies must not be pressed too far. Nevertheless, the pastoral concerns, the developing liturgical practices and the ecclesiastical implications of the "basic communities" make for an instructive comparison with the Methodist movement as it developed in the eighteenth century.

The Preferential Option for the Poor

The preferential option for the poor has been called the trademark of today's Latin American Church. Certainly it is an identifying slogan of Liberation Theology. It means basically two things: looking upon society from the perspective of the poor, the powerless and the marginalised; and giving public witness of solidarity with them in their struggle for liberation. The basic question being responded to is this: What does it mean to be a Christian in a world that knows so much misery? What is the Christian message, what is the shape of Christian existence in the midst of such vast numbers of poor. Poor not only because economic deprivation, but also because such people are considered insignificant?

The orientation is very significant for the direction of Liberation Theology. Two comments would seem to be in order. First, much European and North American theology is concerned with addressing the scepticism of the unbeliever but for Liberation

Theology the focus is not the "unbeliever" but the "non-person." Secondly, although such an orientation has special significance for the Latin American scene it is not confined to it. Such concern has received strong expression in recent Catholic social teaching and was explicitly embraced by the Canadian Conference of Catholic Bishops in their much discussed *Ethical Reflections On the Economic Crisis* of 1983. The bishops began a document by locating the "fundamental Gospel principles" underlying their concerns: "The first principle has to do with the preferential option for the poor, the afflicted and the oppressed....As Christians, we are called to follow Jesus by identifying with the victims of injustice, by analyzing the dominant attitudes and structures that cause human suffering, and by actively supporting the poor and oppressed in their struggles to transform society."[15] That statement is sufficient to remind us that the orientation implied in this slogan may have large significance for Christian living and thinking far beyond Latin America.

Liberation

Of course, no theme is more central to this movement than the theme of liberation itself. Liberation is, however, a very complex term. Gutierrez distinguished three interpenetrating levels of meaning of this central word. First the term expresses the aspiration of oppressed peoples and social classes. It emphasizes the "conflictual aspect" of the process which puts them at odds with oppressive groups and wealthy nations. Secondly on another level, liberation can be applied to an understanding of history. It is a total vision whereby people are freed from the fatalistic view that they can do nothing about their own destiny while at the same time it infuses them with the energy that they can indeed contribute "to the creation of a new man and a qualitatively different society." The third level is liberation from sin through Jesus Christ which leads to a fresh appropriation of the biblical sources as a drama of liberation.[16] While much could be said about the way these levels interpenetrate each other and the largeness of the vision being expressed we will limit ourselves to two comments.

First, the Biblical story of the Exodus experience, the liberation from Egypt, is paradigmatic for Liberation Theology. The Exodus story is, in the memorable phrase of Michael Walzer, "an idea of great presence and power" in Western political and religious thought. It has profound depth in our culture: "Wherever people know the Bible, and experience oppression, the Exodus has sustained their spirits and (sometimes) inspired their resistance."[17] Perhaps no Christian group drew from it such sustaining power and hope, in sermon and song, as did the American blacks from the days of slavery to the present:

> Shout the glad tidings o'er
>   Egypt's dark sea
> Jehovah has triumphed, his people
>   are free.

Our second comment concerns the way in which liberation theologians link the terms salvation and liberation. For Latin American Christians who turn increasingly to Biblical sources, the Exodus story gathers up and focuses an understanding of salvation which embraces and transforms the whole of reality. Liberation theologians do not limit the term salvation to social liberation, but they bring these terms into the closest possible relationship.

Christology

This leads us directly to the question of the role played in Liberation Theology by Jesus Christ. For Christian faith is faith centred in, and shaped by, Jesus Christ as the saving revelation of God. There is a great variety of understandings, ranging from Jesus as the historical model of liberating life to the experience of the risen Christ who gives encouragement and guidance.[18] One of the most fruitful presentations is that of Jon Sobrino in his stimulating book, *Christology at the Crossroads*. Sobrino is emphatic about the Christological center of Christian faith and how that centre shapes our thinking. He states: "...we cannot assume at the start that we already know who God is and move from there...we can only learn who God is from the cross and resurrection of Jesus."[19] Unlike some other liberation theologians, Sobrino focuses his liberating understanding in the cross, in an understanding of the atonement. He puts it this way:

> *The Father suffers the death of the Son and takes upon himself all the pain and suffering of history. In this ultimate solidarity with humanity he reveals himself as the God of love, who opens up a hope and a future through the most negative side of history. Thus Christian existence is nothing else but a process of participating in this same process whereby God loves the world and hence in the very life of God.*[20]

With such a firm theological center, Sobrino can join his fellow liberations theologians in their great interest in the historical Jesus. They are not primarily interested in historical facts but they "regard the historical Jesus as the most satisfactory theological focus for all the different themes in liberation theology."[21] One good reason for their concern is that if the historical Jesus is ignored, our image of God and the nature of divine power may be profoundly distorted. The Christ of dogma, unchecked by constant reference to the historical Jesus, can all too readily be manipulated. God can then be conceived as "omnipotent" and "omniscient" but he ceases to be the God who is "with us" and "for us" in Jesus Christ. Our understanding of the power of God will be dramatically different when our image of divine power is shaped by the historical Jesus and "the slain lamb of God" than when it is shaped by notions of kingly power derived from the Roman, Spanish or Portuguese empires.

Recurring Questions

Liberation Theology is not only a significant movement. It has also generated much debate and controversy. Attention must first be given to two recurring questions.

Is Liberation Theology Marxist?

The first question concerns the degree to which Liberation Theology is inspired by Marxism. Some critics charge that Liberation Theology has capitulated to Marxism or is in danger of doing so. What are we to say to this? We may begin by hearing the recent responses of some of the most distinguished of liberation theologians. The brothers Boff (Leonardo and Clodovis) have replied to this charge in a recent work that:

> This myth is not easy to dispel....But we must make the attempt. Let us state, once and for all, frankly and unambiguously: by no means is Marxism the moving force, basis, or inspiration of the theology of liberation. Christian faith is. It is the Gospel that is the determining qualifier of the theology of liberation, as it must be of any theology. The Gospel is the heart....When Marxism is used at all, it is used only *partially* and *instrumentally*.[22]

In an interview given for the *National Catholic Reporter* (31 October 1986) Gutierrez responded to this question in a similar vein: "There is no direct relationship between liberation theology and Marxism. But in liberation theology, we use social science...[and] today, it is impossible to analyze the situations of poor countries without some Marxist notions." Gregory Baum in an article entitled "Liberation Theology and Marxism" has engaged the issue directly and at some length. His conclusion is "that liberation theology has engaged in critical dialogue with Marxism, that it has enriched, through this dialogue, the understanding of biblical categories and Christian doctrine, but that its reliance on Marxism is only in the area of social analysis, and even there this reliance is tangential."[23] William R. Barr, Protestant theologian, emphasizes that there is a vigorous debate "within liberation theology as to the usefulness of Marxist analysis in coming to grips with the contemporary reality of Latin America." He concludes that "what these Latin American liberationists call for is neither a wholesale acceptance nor rejection of Marxism but a *critical appropriation* of Marxist analysis within a Christian vision of human life and the world."[24] This would seem to be an accurate and sober assessment.

Violence

A quite persistent charge is that liberation theologians support violence. One must look at the reality of violence within Latin American society. The Methodist theologian, José Miguez-Bonino, has strongly asserted that we cannot discuss this matter as an abstract question as to whether we approve or will take part in violence. Such a possibility does not exist in that situation. The question is not one of non-violence "but of the kinds, forms and limits of violence present in a conflict involving oppression and liberation."[25] There are three types of violence marking the current situation: (1) the institutionalized violence of the present social order; (2) the overt repressive violence which defends this order; and (3) some counter violence on the part of the oppressed. In varying degrees these three forms pervade society. It is an agonizing situation, one in which it is extremely difficult to be wise. Christians down through the ages, however, have known what it is to decide that some form of counter violence had to be resorted to when all other processes had failed and when it had become clear that to refrain would perpetuate a greater injustice than to overthrow the tyrannical order.

Robert McAfee Brown reports an incident that is worth repeating:

> I once moderated a panel in which Gustavo and a well known pacifist debated the issue of violence in Christian ethics. The pacifist had ready responses for every question; he had answered them so often that there was no pain, no anguish. Gustavo dealt with each question with pain and anguish. He wrestled with the moral dilemma that Christians might find that all other alternatives to

violence had been exhausted. There were no pat answers. It was an ongoing struggle he shared with his listeners. It was authentic.[26]

Liberation theologians are not violent people, they do not glorify violence, they are keenly aware of the evils that attend it, they have themselves suffered terribly from violence. But when one is engaged in a revolution to overthrow oppression, violence cannot simply be ruled out in advance.

Critique

There are, however, serious limitations in Latin American Liberation Theology. Frequently, the criticism has been made in general terms to the effect that it is thin, lacking in professional depth and range. Criticism needs, however, to be more precise.

The most serious weakness of Liberation Theology lies in a cluster of issues that are not marginal, but actually central, to its own concern. This cluster of issues may be grouped under the heading of theological ethics.

Despite its passionate, moral commitment, Liberation Theology is marked by an almost total neglect of theological ethics and this deprives it of the intellectual stability and precision to make it truly persuasive. A vagueness in both its social analysis and theological structure robs it of the strength that will be needed especially in a time of social reconstruction. Liberation Theology moves from the presentation of its Biblical themes and its historical vision directly to politics without passing through ethics. This makes for a very serious deficiency because if we are to make informed judgments between different courses of actions, then we need the guidance of a developed social ethics. As James Gustafson has stated, there are great resources in traditional political concepts which would bring about a needed precision in both their "indictments of present social conditions and clearer prescriptions about the social conditions that ought to prevail as a result of the social changes they seek to foster."[27] Such a resource, it should be added, would bring not only a needed precision to liberation thought, it would also help build in principles of self-criticism, the lack of which makes Liberation Theology vulnerable to ideological captivity. Such a resource of self-criticism will be of particular importance in a period of social reconstruction, after liberation has been achieved, because the basic test of the quality of a people's liberty remains, as Edmund Burke long ago observed, the use that is made of power.

The neglect of ethics is but part of the wider neglect of theological anthropology, or a sustained analysis of human nature in the light of Christian understanding. All our ethical theory is profoundly shaped by our understanding of human nature, of what human beings are and are not capable of, the nature of their illusions and self-deceptions, their possibilities and their limits, the creative and the destructive consequences of freedom upon their communities. A theological anthropology delineating such matters profoundly shapes social ethics.

One of the great strengths of the Christian Realism of Reinhold Niebuhr was the clarity and depth of his understanding of human nature which he brought to bear upon a wide range of social issues. Terms like "sin" and "grace" became meaningful categories for interpreting both personal and social experience. Throughout his voluminous writings he showed that the Biblical understanding of human nature was a profounder basis for democratic life than the understanding which had informed bourgeois society. He also demonstrated how this theological anthropology formed the basis for unmasking the deceptions and illusions to which America in her "precarious eminence" seemed peculiarly prone. Moreover, the Biblical understanding of the transcendence of God serves in his thought as a vantage point of judgment in which human activities can be seen in their value, limitations and corruptions. Christian realism also lifts up the way in which a distinctive Christian doctrines such as the work of Christ...the historic doctrine of the atonement...sheds further light on the complexity of human beings, our grandeur and our misery, while at the same time revealing the divine love that forgives our sins, heals the springs of our affections, and thus lays the foundation of new life. In a word, the centre of the Christian message shapes the basis for the combination of realism and hope, so desperately needed by our world. This understanding of human nature is thoroughly integrated in Niebuhr's thought with an explication of the work of Christ and in such a way as to shape an ethical analysis that could inform public policy.

It is this kind of theological and ethical analysis which is lacking in Liberation Theology. Consequently it sometimes means that the transcendence norm of judgement, which builds in the principle of self criticism, and which relativizes all social programmes and visions, is lost or obscured. It is this which makes the movement vulnerable to cultural or ideological captivity. Likewise the failure of much of Liberation Theology to do its thinking from key central Christian doctrines means that the *distinctive* contribution of the Christian insight into human nature and the dynamics of history are not brought to bear upon a public philosophy. Instead, the distinctly Christian contribution tends to be limited to providing motivation, energy and a communal basis for the realization of the vision of the new society. This is the deficiency which lends substance to Schubert Ogden's criticism that liberation theologies tend to collapse the meaning of theology into witness.[28]

Conclusion

We began by saying that the appearance of Liberation Theology constituted the most momentous development on the theological scene of the past two decades. Whatever may be our final assessment, the achievements of this theological movement are already significant. Liberation theologians have reminded us all that the concept of full liberation is central both to theology and Christian life and that, important as both existentialism and pietism have been, such views of salvation were conceived in a too individualistic way. Like the Protestant Social Gospel before it, liberation theologies forcefully remind us of the social substance of all personal existence. Liberation Theology has also reminded us of the prophetic power of much of the Biblical witness and also of the relevance of many prophetic strands in the Christian heritage that have often been neglected. Not least of all this movement reminds us just how costly Christian witness and thought can be. In the past ten years "at least a thousand priests and religious have been martyred."[29] Through these people the ancient saying that "the blood of the martyrs is the seed of the church" is taking on fresh and powerful meaning in our time. Their witness has contributed notably to the heritage of the Church which sustains us all.

The centre of the debate currently taking place in all the churches is the relationship of faith and society, Christ and culture. Liberation Theology may not always have adequate, let alone final, answers to that grand question and unending quest. It is, however, a very important theological movement in a region that is critical for the future of Christianity. The humaneness of its vision, the quality of its thought and the sacrifice of its leaders evoke our gratitude and command our attention.

Notes

1. Penny Lernoux, "The Long Path to Puebla," in John Eagleson and Philip Scharper eds., *Puebla and Beyond.* (Maryknoll, N.Y.: Orbis Books, 1979), 3.

2. Ibid., 4.

3. Ibid., 5.

4. Ibid., 9.

5. Medellin Document on "Peace" in Joseph Gremillion, *The Gospel of Peace and Justice: Catholic Social Teaching Since Pope John* (Maryknoll, N.Y.: Orbis Books, 1976), 462.

6. Lernoux, "The Long Path to Puebla," 17 ff.

7. Ibid., 19ff.

8. Gregory Baum, "Liberation Theology and Marxism,"*The Ecumenist*, 25 no. 2 (January/February 1987): 22.

9. Moises Sandoval, "Report From the Conference," in *Puebla and Beyond*, 31.

10. Ibid., 36.

11. Robert McAfee Brown, *Gustavo Gutiérrez* (Atlanta: John Knox Press, 1980), 18.

12. Leonardo Boff, *Ecclesiogenesis: The Base Communities Reinvent the Church* (Maryknoll, N.Y.: Orbis Books, 1986), 11.

13. Ibid., 12.

14. Ibid., 13.

15. "Ethical Reflections on the Economic Crisis," in John R. Williams, ed., *Canadian Churches and Social Justice* (Toronto: Anglican Book Centre and James Lorimer, 1984), 88f.

16. See Gustavo Gutierrez, *A Theology of Liberation* (Maryknoll, N.Y.: Orbis Books, 1973), 36ff.

17. Michael Walzer, *Exodus and Revolution* (New York: Basic Books, 1985), ix, 4.

18. See William R. Barr, "Debated Issues in Liberation Theology," in *Theology Today* (January 1987).

19. Jon Sobrino, S.J., *Christology at the Crossroads* (Maryknoll, N.Y.: Orbis Books, 1978), 240.

20. Ibid., 224.

21. Ibid., 274.

22. Leonardo Boff & Clodovis Boff, *Liberation Theology From Confrontation to Dialogue* (San Francisco: Harper and Row, 1986), 22.

23. Baum, "Liberation Theology and Marxism," 26.

24. Barr, "Debated Issues...", 516, 519.

25. José Miguez-Bonino, "Violence: A Theological Reflection," in Gerald F. Anderson & Thomas F. Stransky, C.S.P., eds., *Mission Trends No. 3*, (New York: Paulist Press; Grand Rapids: Wm. B. Eerdmans, 1976), 125.

26. McAfee Brown, *Gustavo Gutiérrez*, 26.

27. James Gustafson, *Ethics From A Theocentric Perspective* (Chicago: University of Chicago Press, 1981), vi 73.

28. See Schubert Ogden, *Faith and Freedom: Toward a Theology of Liberation* (Nashville: Abingdon, 1979), 33ff. See also the debate this occasioned with Dorothy Soelle in Brian Mahan & L. Dale Richesin, eds., *The Challenge of Liberation Theology* (Maryknoll, N.Y.: Orbis Books, 1984).

29. Theo Witvliet, *A Place in the Sun: An Introduction to Liberation Theology in the Third World* (Maryknoll, N.Y.: Orbis Books, 1985), 132.

CHAPTER FOUR

CHRISTIAN FAITH AND THE
SOCIAL TASK

We began this
discussion of the relation between Christian faith and society by
noting that the topic is a matter of widespread controversy in
Christian churches everywhere. We acknowledged that the debate
is sometimes fierce and frequently confused and urged that this
should occasion no surprise because it is a complex debate
concerned with issues of great importance. In many ways the
debate is evidence of the vitality of the Church. The debate is
important. It concerns the nature and range of the missions of the
Church in a rapidly changing world and the kinds of witness
appropriate to that mission. The debate is set in a global context;
it has to do with what it means to belong to the Christian community
in a world where fellow believers are faced with vastly different
social issues. It involves our understanding of salvation, God's
relation to the world, the nature and range of the redemptive work
of Jesus Christ. The debate is decisive for our view of Christian
social ethics. We urged that it is all this because the controversy

over the relationship between faith and society, Christ and culture, is at bottom a discussion about the nature of the Christian faith itself.

In order to bring the debate into focus we have discussed some of the major movements of recent times — the Social Gospel, Christian Realism, Evangelicalism, Fundamentalism and Liberation Theology. All of these movements have engaged the issue with energy and considerable social consequence. They illustrate the range and nature of living options. Their different approaches form the context for our own engagement of the issue.

The conviction which has informed these pages is that those central doctrines of Christian faith — Incarnation, Atonement and Justification by Grace — which are usually related only to our personal quests for forgiveness, renewal and meaning, are also the basis for the most adequate social or political theology. It follows from this that if Christian thinking proceeds from this centre, it will be able to emphasize that there are dimensions of the faith which transcend all social and political concern and involvement but which, at the same time, do justice to the fact that faith is related to all aspects of our communal life. The centre of the faith provides us with a resource of insight and healing that can help us to keep the personal and social dimensions of life together and whole, and in doing so transcend the debilitating reduction and distortions represented by those wretched contemporary words - politicization and privatization.

It would be wise, however, before attempting to articulate such positive resources, to acknowledge that Christians throughout history have shown that there are certain pitfalls to which they have been particularly prone, and which are again proving attractive. It is always well to acknowledge the truth of Reinhold Niebuhr's remark that "Christians are frequently a source of confusion rather than light when dealing with large social issues." Quite often Christians forget that zeal and concern are one thing, knowledge and wisdom quite another. Moreover each of these pitfalls to which Christians seem so prone has been related to a significant failure in theological understanding. It might, therefore, be instructive, first to glance at these pitfalls which have proved to be attractive.

Pitfalls

The first is one that makes a sharp division, even separation, between the personal life of faith and social concern. This view regards religion as concerned with individual integrity, the cultivation of personal graces, and indeed all the fruits of the spirit, in terms of personal relationships. But anything pertaining to laws, customs and political structures is considered as belonging to the realm of politics and as such beyond either the scrutiny or concern of faith. The Christian "ought not to meddle" as the phrase goes.

Nowhere on this continent was this understanding developed with such completeness as it was in the American South prior to the Civil War. All churches were involved in setting forth this position, but it was developed with particular learning and brilliance by the theologians of the Southern Presbyterian Church. The context for elaboration of this view was slavery. The core of the argument set forth was that the *institution* of slavery was a political question, not a moral or religious issue. Religious concern, they argued, was restricted to the *relation* of the master and the slave, and they were concerned that such a relation should be as humane as possible. The institution of slavery itself was considered to be beyond the range of religious concern. The great complexity of the ethical issues that Christians faced in that particular context must be acknowledged but the designation of the institution of slavery as a political matter beyond the range of religious concern was certainly a fatal turning point with long-reaching consequences. Indeed, as late as the 1960s, basically the same arguments were advanced in defence of segregation. This example is used not in order that we might feel superior or self-righteous. Quite the contrary. These Southern Presbyterians are a good example of the attractiveness of this pitfall because they combined exceptional intellectual power with a personal piety and devotion marked by great intensity and beauty. Nevertheless, such an approach to the issue meant that the full range of the Lordship of God, over the whole of life was effectively obscured.[1]

The second pitfall is that Christians are frequently inclined to sentimentalize social issues. This may not be as true as it was in the early decades of this century, but it recurs with sufficient frequency to merit noting. Christians have sometimes also failed to face the fact that serious imbalances of power in the community are always productive of injustice. This failure to come to grips with the structural problems of the community often issues in the substitution of charity for justice. Now philanthropy is important; no society is healthy without the generous spirit of which philanthropy is an expression. But it should be recognized that philanthropy by itself is the concession of the strong to the weak in such a way that the basis of the power of the strong is not called into question. It is thus easy to sentimentalize the social issue by failing to come to grips with the injustice which attends serious imbalances of power. Sometimes Christians dwell so much on motives and attitudes that they do not clearly face the fact that justice is not to be secured or maintained without the use of the instruments of power, instruments which are always ambiguous. Christians are frequently, and understandably, motivated by a concern for moral purity and an aversion to conflict and these concerns sometimes tempt us to sentimental analysis and unrealistic strategies in engaging social problems. The sentimentalizing of complex social issues is a pitfall to which Christians have sometimes been prone.

The third pitfall takes various forms, but may be designated, to use the contemporary jargon, by the term politicization. In addition to being a linguistic monstrosity, the content of the term is not as readily arrived at as might be assumed. In general, however, whenever the Christian faith is simply and directly identified with a specific political order, cause or programme, then a politicization of faith has taken place. It takes place across the whole political spectrum. The activities of the New Religious Right, as exemplified by Moral Majority in the last two American presidential elections, can serve as an example on the political right. On the other hand, politicization is the charge that Edward Norman has brought against what someone has called the unholy alliance between trendy theologians and chic social activists. Latin American Liberation Theology, the World Council of Churches (especially its Program to Combat Racism), and those involved in the struggle against apartheid in South Africa are among those whom Norman regards as most guilty. His charge is that Christianity is being "reinterpreted as a scheme of social and political action, dependent, it is true, upon supernatural authority for its ultimate claims to attention, but rendered in categories that are derived from the political theories and practices of contemporary society." The criticism he makes is not directed at some unfortunate detail. On the contrary, such politicization he regards as involving nothing less than "the internal transformation of the faith itself."[2]

Norman's critique is not convincing because he really criticizes the politicization on the Left from the standpoint of a politicization on the Right, by way of a quite radical separation of faith from social concern. Nevertheless, we can agree with him that politicization is a real threat today. The threat appears both in social and religious terms. First, politicized Christianity, both right and left, ends up absolutizing relative values, a process which is always productive of the most virulent of evils. Such politicization is an expression of the Biblical meaning of idolatry. The evil of such idolatrous faith is virulent because it is disguised as devotion to values. No one worships an obvious golden calf to say nothing of an obvious irrelevance! We worship values, the values of nation, race, class, and culture — and these can be very important values — but the point is that they are worshipped in such a way that they are effectively removed both from divine judgment and human dissent. Politicized religion — and that is the essence of idolatry — thus represents a danger to society. Moreover, when the tension between the transcendent dimensions of our faith and the great causes which must command our energies is loosened, then the very nature of Christian faith is obscured, and with it its true relevance to both our personal and social life. Politicization of the faith is thus both socially dangerous because of the way it absolutizes relative values, and religiously enervating because such a utilitarian approach empties the transcendent dimensions of the faith of their meaning and power.

These then are three pitfalls confronting us — radical separation, the sentimentalizing of social issues, and politicization. But such a locating of perils serves only to bring to the centre of the stage the grand old question: What *is* the relationship between our ultimate religious commitment and our pursuit of social and cultural values? Our approach to this issue may be indicated by briefly discussing a few matters at the heart of the Christian message.

Resources

Human Nature
Surely the realism of the Christian understanding of human nature can prove to be a significant resource for all who seek to face the rapidly changing world with a steady eye. Anyone immersed in the Christian understanding of humankind ought never to be surprised by evil. The Christian understanding resists not only obvious evils such as the grasping for tyrannical power and the exploitation of the weak, but it ought also to make us particularly alert to the way in which the good can become stale if it is not kept open to that divine judgment which is also the spring of renewal. The Christian understanding of human nature is the kind of resource that gives us a lively sense of what Reinhold Niebuhr called "ironic evil," by which he meant the tendency for our virtue to become vice, our strength to become weakness and our wisdom to become folly whenever pretension stretches them beyond their limits.

The Judaeo-Christian understanding of human nature has a deep appreciation of the uniqueness and worth of the person. Now, of course, Christians have no corner on either the affirmation or the defence of the dignity of the person. The significance of the Biblical view is that it locates our dignity in the position we hold before God. Our relationship to God, in this understanding, is not something added on to our being, as an option or as an extra, but is constitutive of our being. Such a relationship, which is the very life of faith, can provide a significant leverage over the political order, and that is a matter of great significance in this technological age which facilitates such concentrations of power.

Christians, however, know not only the reality of sin but equally the reality of grace, and that means that we should always be alert to the possibility of the new in history. People informed by the Christian understanding are realists. Their understanding of sin makes them realists. They agree with realists generally that self-interest is a fundamental datum of all collective life. However, they are not cynics. They do not believe that self-interest is the only thing operating in life. They know, value and nurture the human capacity to reach out in care and concern. Knowing both these things they also know that the mark of leadership, or statesmanship, is the capacity to find the points of coincidence between the group or national interest and the needs and interests of the wider human community. Moreover, Christians live in the assurance that God is one who ever goes before them, opening the doors to the new. In a word, the Christian understanding of human nature is a source of insight for us because it provides such a balanced assessment of both the creative and disruptive effects of our freedom upon our communities.

Both aspects need to be emphasized. The creative goodness of the human spirit, the access to being that we gain through personal relationships, needs to be lifted up in this age when the quantitative measure has gained such wide acceptance. But equally, any realistic analysis of the human condition must rigorously come to grips with the manner in which our existence is separated from what we essentially are, or are meant to be with that condition of the soul that we call sin, which is deeper than our conscious choices and intentions. It is recognised that we cannot be made whole again without some understanding of the broken situation in which we exist. There is a profundity in the Christian understanding of human nature that can be a much needed resource for us today. So it was not surprising to see the political philosopher, Kenneth Thompson, as he pondered the resources available for a wise foreign policy, remarking that "Christian realism by illuminating the misery and grandeur of man can be a textbook for the diplomatist. (For) it can rid men of their illusions while preparing them for their 'finest hours'."[3]

This heritage is not only a resource of insight but also a resource of *spirit*. By this is meant not only a general good will and kind feelings but rather that religious faith nurtured by a Biblical understanding of human nature ought to be productive of a peculiar quality of spirit that is a needed resource for the complexity of these days. What is the character of that spirit? It is a *combination* of resolution in the face of evil and a humility born of the knowledge that our cause, however right, however just, is not absolute. It is a tall order. Moral resolution and humility do not commonly travel together. This combination is especially difficult for participants in conflict. Yet one of the greatest examples in history was just such a central participant in a terrible conflict — Abraham Lincoln. He was a leader who, in the midst of the conflict of civil war, was richly informed by the Biblical view of human nature and the spirit which flowed from it. *He was resolute.* He was much more resolute than his generals as the Southern Confederacy, to its chagrin, was to learn. He was resolved: (1) to preserve the union; and (2) to abolish slavery. But his resolution was combined with a humility that came with the knowledge that although his cause was relatively right, it was not absolute. It had been corrupted. It had been corrupted not only by Yankee self-interest but more importantly by the moral pretension that usually tempts the advocates of righteous causes. The combination of resolution and humility was what was so important and so rare. Lincoln did not allow his resolution, his moral commitment, to lead him into self-righteousness or moral rigidity. Nor, on the other hand, did he allow his great capacity for compassion to betray him into weakness or a sentimental analysis of the situation or the strategies necessary to deal with it. Reinhold Niebuhr's comment on Lincoln is pertinent to our discussion:

> This combination of resolution about the immediate issues with a religious awareness of another dimension of meaning and judgement must be regarded as almost a perfect model of the difficult but not impossible task of remaining loyal and responsible toward the moral treasures of a free civilization on the one hand while yet having some religious vantage point over the struggle.[4]

Lincoln remains not only a relevant example of wise political leadership in the midst of a terrible conflict but also an example of the perennial relevance of Biblical insight into human nature. He gave expression to a perspective and a spirit peculiarly needed in our own time if we are to articulate an understanding that transcends both the doomsayers and the techno-fixers.

The Distinctive Centre

This perspective leads us directly to the distinctive centre of the Christian message with its arresting proclamation. The message carried to the world the astonishing affirmation that at one and the same place, or more precisely, in one and the same person, there is the revelation of the unfathomable depth of God's suffering, sin-bearing love *and* the actualization, the coming to expression, of true humanity in which love and freedom have met and become one. It was the sort of announcement that took one's breath away and so we find St. Paul exclaiming about the "inexhaustible" or "unsearchable" riches of Christ, and we find the ancient creeds of the church declaring that in Him we meet Very God and Very Man. And in our own time that wonderful detective novelist, Dorothy L. Sayers, would characteristically remark, "Now we may call that doctrine exhilarating or we may call it devastating; we may call it revelation or we may call it rubbish, but if we call it dull, then words have no meaning."[5]

This vibrant core of the Christian message has always been full of significance for people in their personal quests for meaning, forgiveness and renewal. It will ever remain so. My conviction, however, is that it is precisely this same centre that can illuminate and hold together both the personal and social dimensions of Christian faith in ways peculiarly relevant to our contemporary debate. The relevance of these basic affirmations to our social as well as our personal lives may be illustrated in three ways. First, by showing the relevance of the "evangelical" doctrine of Justification by Grace for a political ethic; secondly, by indicating the relevance of this centre for the question of tolerance in a pluralist society; and thirdly by demonstrating importance of the Christological affirmation for the joining together of a sober realism and the energies of hope.

Justification by Grace and a Political Ethic

We are a generation who live daily with tragic choices. Every statesman, for example, is daily faced with trying to realize partially incompatible goals. Being responsible often means making the choice of suppressing one value in order to secure or preserve another. Moreover, the very struggle to secure justice itself involves the use of the instruments of power, and the instruments of power are always ambiguous. Nor can innocence be maintained, or purity achieved, by withdrawing from the struggle. The fact to be recognized is this: *there is no moral hiding place.* It is precisely here that we see the genius of Christian faith. The central symbol of that faith is the Cross of Christ. That cross discloses the tragic depths of life, the pervasiveness of human sin. It does this through the same reconciling act of God in Christ which provides resources to cope with those tragic realities. Now the term Justification by Grace means the process by which we are made right with God, by which we are reconciled to God. Moreover, the heart of the Christian experience is that the grace we meet in Christ both illumines the depth of our need and is a power to reconcile us. Individual believers across the centuries have known what it means to experience the subtlety and depth of sin through an appropriation of the grace that brought both forgiveness and the energies of new life. Our contention is that this basic doctrine is of great social significance. To act socially in terms of Justification by Grace is to know three things: (1) that the Divine Love that has met us, impels us to seek a greater justice in the community; (2) that the same Divine Love that impels us to justice also illumines the sin we will be involved in by our efforts; (3) this doctrine also assures us of a resource of mercy to cover the evil we do in order to be responsible. This is a perspective that saves us both from a paralysis of will *and* the pretension to which our righteous causes usually tempts us. It bids us seek the combination embodied in Lincoln — a spirit of resolution against evil with an awareness of "the taint of sin in the cause of our devotion." Clearly, whenever the ambiguity of political decisions and the tragic dimensions of history are obscured, the full relevance of this Christian understanding will be lost.

This happened in the United States in the mid-nineteenth century. Indeed to read much of the theology of that period, to say nothing of the literature of social and political conflict, is to be left wondering, what happened to this cardinal doctrine of the Reformation. It was present of course, but one has the feeling that it was there because it was supposed to be there. After all, the doctrine is an important part of the Christian heritage and theological discourse would be incomplete without it. It was, not informing religious thought and life in any vital way. Surely one of the reasons why it was not is that those who affirmed it failed to bring it into a living engagement with the great social issues of the day. That was a great pity for if ever Christians needed whatever resources of insight and healing there were in Christian faith to engage the ambiguous values and tragic choices of communal life, it was that time and place.

We have already alluded to this tumultuous period in American life — to the argument that religion was concerned only with the *relation* of the master and the slave, not with the *institution* of slavery; and to the way in which Lincoln, unlike most of the churchmen of his day, drew upon the riches of insight and spirit inhering in the Biblical understanding of human nature. Sustained study of this upheaval in American life could be of immense value for Christians because it is one the finest historical examples we have for dealing with the issue of Christian faith and society.

When the debates which Christians had over the issue of slavery are considered the thought will not go away that a vital understanding of this evangelical doctrine of Justification by Grace could have been both illuminating and healing in this tragic situation. Why? Because the doctrine does two things simultaneously. It points to the riches of Divine Love which throws a searchlight into the depths of the evil in which we are involved. At the same time, the doctrine points to the resources of grace enabling us to cope responsibly with a difficult situation. It really is a doctrine that is indispensable for dealing with the tragic choices of life. Therein lies both its truth and its relevance. It could have enabled those Christians to have said something like this: We know that we are involved in an evil situation. We know also that there is now no easy kind of solution. But we are serious about getting rid of this evil; we will set a realistic timetable to show our resolution, and we know that there are resources of grace to cover the evil we will be involved in, through our attempts to be responsible and just. However, they did not say that sort of thing. The reason they did not do so would seem to be because moralism had become the content of their Christian understanding obscuring the depths of both sin and grace. This ingrained moralism meant that they felt they must always be righteous, supporting righteous causes, instead of being forgiven sinners coping as best they could with an entrenched social evil in an ethically complex situation. The result was most instructive and we have seen similar results scores of times: *they deceived themselves, so that things could no longer be called by their proper names.* So slavery was no longer condemned as an evil, as it had previously been in the South; it was now even declared to be a "positive good." This failure was not simply a failure of courage. It was a theological failure. It meant that the depths of both sin and grace, and consequently the social meaning of the doctrine of Justification by Grace, were obscured by the all-pervading moralism. This meant that when the conflict was joined in bloody civil war, this moralistic understanding, instead of illuminating the tragic dimensions of the conflict, served rather to intensify the crusading self-righteous moralism of both sides in the conflict.

The doctrine of Justification by Grace does not mean that we do not take sides in the struggle for social values. It does not say, "A plague on all your houses." It does not say that "since sin abounds, no significant distinctions are to be made." This is the fear expressed by Juan Louis Segundo. He fears that this "relativization of any and every political system" will end up "being a politically neutral theology" lacking the enthusiasm necessary for significant social change.[6] NO! It is not an invitation to neutrality. But it does mean that the very faith that impels us to action also keeps us aware of the fact that our cause, though perhaps relatively righteous, is not absolute. This awareness will not get rid of conflict but it will mitigate the ferocity of the struggle in which we are and must be engaged if treasured social values are to be secured and preserved. This emphasis upon the transcendent dimensions of divine grace is neither an excuse, nor a summons, to escape history. Quite the contrary. In the words of Reinhold Niebuhr, "It gives us a fulcrum from which we can operate in history. It gives us a faith by which we can seek to fulfill our historic tasks without illusions and without despair."[7]

Christian Conviction, Tolerance and a Pluralistic Society

We live in a pluralistic society and we treasure the values of pluralism. We are also keenly aware of the potential that strong religious convictions have for disrupting public discourse, of the danger such persuasions can pose for a pluralistic society. History is full of the evils that attend the giving of divine sanction to particular positions and relative values. This is the peril that follows upon the politicization of faith. On the other hand we are also keenly aware of how a religious void in the public life, a "naked public square," can easily be filled with its opposite — an intolerant absolutism. Our situation then, of being members of a pluralistic society which we treasure, and alive to the perils of both politicization and that emptiness in which nothing is seriously valued, raises for us an important question: How do we combine deep religious conviction with an open, tolerant spirit? It is a question all serious believers must face and it is a question that is important for the wider community.

The question drives Christians right back to their centre. Indeed this question about a tolerant spirit will reveal as quickly as any the real nature of what it is we really believe. The question is, "What is the nature of the truth we affirm?" Christians answer that the truth they affirm concerns the Divine Love revealed in Jesus Christ. It is the basic content of Christian faith. *But that content also shapes the way we should hold our faith and the way we witness to it.* It means that a Gospel of Grace cannot properly be witnessed to gracelessly. The content of the truth to which we witness shapes the manner in which we witness to it. It can be truth *in* us only when we know it is a truth *over* us, in judgment and mercy. Indeed whenever Christians have sought coercively to impose their faith, they have been really concerned not with witnessing to God's love, but with the power to impose. The nature of the truth to which Christians testify — the immensity of the Divine Love — means that we can have great confidence in the truth to which we witness but only a broken confidence in the adequacy of our understanding of it.

Realism and Hope
There is one other matter commanding our attention. Everywhere people are crying out from the depths of wounded spirits. It does

not matter where we live or what our occupation is. There is enough pain and sorrow in any city block to crack the heart of the world. This is a point where blunt speech is appropriate. Sensitive people in our time cannot be interested in Christian faith if it is unable to cope with suffering or come to grips with the tragic dimensions of life. But that, it seems to me, is precisely the genius of Christian faith. The Cross is its central symbol. It is the symbol not only of the Christ who once upon a time climbed the hill of Golgotha, but the symbol of the Christ who is *ever* coming out from the heart of God to be *with* us, and *for* us and (however faintly), the power of new life *in* us.

This means that the Christian message is marked by realism and hope for it is a proclamation concerning a Lord who is both *crucified* and *risen*. We know that the forces of depersonalization and destruction are potent. They are everywhere around us and within us. In this age of incredible technological power, unless all the forces of human community are nurtured, the human prospect is indeed a grim one. Nevertheless, in the midst of all this, the Christian lives with the energies of hope, a hope that is not born of innocence or based on some rootless, idealistic fantasy. On the contrary, Christian hope is grounded in the reality, purpose and power of God. Christians have been claimed by a vision, what they call "the kingdom of God." The vision is that humanity in its wholeness is humanity in true community. Moreover, Christians are assured that this vision is rooted in the purpose of God, that the ultimate moral purpose and hope are ontologically grounded. That is why in the face of even intractable problems, we can be summoned to lift up our hearts.

Certainly this faith has profound meaning for individuals. But just as the individual before God is kept from being sentimental by the reality of sin, and from despair by the largeness of God's mercy, so this centre of the faith promises that combination of realism and hope that is at once the fruit of Biblical faith and the perennial need of society.

Conclusion

A debate is raging in the churches. Sometimes it is fierce and frequently it is confused. It is a complex debate and it is concerned with issues of large importance. The centre of the debate is the relationship between faith and society, Christ and culture, and at bottom the debate concerns the nature of Christianity itself.

There are those in our churches who are primarily concerned with the depths, vitality and inwardness of personal Christian experience. They know and deeply value the goodness of God's grace to them. They have known what it means to have life turned around and changed from something stale and aimless into "a life in Christ" that is joyous, meaningful and venturesome. That is always an occasion for rejoicing. Sometimes, however, these newly awakened lives are divorced from concern for the poor and the oppressed of the world. Love has been emptied of the concern for justice, and when that occurs, it has not reached out to the wholeness of human beings.

On the other hand, there are those who have a passionate, at times almost a professional, Christian social concern. They believe, and they are right, that the word justice belongs to the Christian faith as much as forgiveness and redemption. We owe them much. However, sometimes the insight, depth and guidance provided by the doctrines and symbols of the faith are lacking; sometimes the ultimate issues and mysteries of life receive short shrift. And the word needs to be spoken that Christ is no abstract principle but is the One who is *ever* coming out from the heart of God to be with us and for us in the stuff of daily life to claim our minds and to cleanse the springs of our affections.

These two concerns should never be split because they both have their home and lodging in the Present Lordship of the crucified Christ. In the Cross, the inexhaustible symbol of Christianity, the forgiving, healing love of God meets us through One who was rejected and oppressed. In this grand affirmation - the life giving centre of our heritage - the current fractious debate may find creative resolution and the Church be brought to the springs of renewal.

Notes

1. For a discussion of this view of the church see Ernest Trice Thompson, *The Spirituality of the Church: A Distinctive Doctrine of the Presbyterian Church in the United States*, (Richmond, Va.: John Knox Press, 1961).

2. Edward Norman, *Christianity and the World Order* (Oxford: Oxford University Press, 1979), 2.

3. Kenneth Thompson, "Prophets and Politics," *Christianity and Crisis*, 16 May 1955, 61.

4. Reinhold Niebuhr, *The Irony of American History* (New York: Charles Scribner's Sons, 1952), 172.

5. Dorothy L. Sayers, "The Greatest Drama Ever Staged," in *Creed or Chaos* (London: Methuen, 1947), 5.

6. Juan Louis Segundo, S.J., *The Liberation of Theology* (New York: Orbis Books, 1985), 145.

7. Reinhold Niebuhr, "Christian Otherworldliness," *Christianity and Society* 9, no. 1 (Winter 1943): 12.